You Only Need Permission from Yourself.

Jaynette M. Lancaster

Copyright © 2025

All Rights Reserved

Library of Congress Control Number: 2025923767

ISBN: 979-8-9938808-5-3 (trade)

ISBN: 979-8-9938808-1-5 (ebook)

Dedication

To every woman who's ever been told she had to wait for permission…

To the cycle-breakers, the midnight criers, the ones who kept showing up even when no one clapped…

To the girl I used to be and the grown woman I've become…

This is for **YOU.**

For the mothers, daughters, sisters, and survivors.

For the strong ones who still feel deeply.

For the soft ones who've had to be hard to survive.

For every soul who dared to believe that healing is possible and wholeness is their birthright.

This book is your mirror, your reminder, your *permission slip.*

You don't need to earn it. You don't need to beg for it. You only need to give it to yourself.

And now that you have…

Walk in it.

Acknowledgments

To GOD—thank You for being my anchor, my source, and my constant reminder that I was chosen, even when I felt forgotten. You kept me when I couldn't keep myself. Every page in this book is a praise offering for the grace that carried me through.

To my Son—my greatest motivation and my biggest blessing. You gave me purpose long before I understood my own power. Watching you grow gave me the courage to rise, to dream again, and to never stop becoming.

To my Parents—thank you for raising me with love, boundaries, and vision. For allowing me to cry, to question, and to be. Your protection gave me peace. Your structure gave me strength. Because of you, I know how to love with truth and lead with heart.

To every Woman who's ever had to push through while holding it all together—this book was written with you in mind. You are not invisible. You are not too much. You are not behind. You are sacred. You are seen. And you are worthy of the softness you keep giving to everyone else.

To the Village—friends who gave rides, spoke life, held space, and refused to let me quit. You know who you are. Your love wasn't just timely—it was divine.

To every therapist, mentor, my Sisters, stranger, and soul who reminded me that I wasn't alone: thank you. Your words, your witness, your warmth helped me heal in places I didn't know were still aching.

And to the younger me—the 14-year-old girl who didn't think she'd see 15… this one's for you. You lived. You loved. You wrote. And you made it out with your heart still open.

This book is a testimony. A mirror. A permission slip.

Thank you for being a part of my journey.

About the Author

Jaynette Lancaster is the voice behind the victories and the vulnerability in these pages. A real estate advisor, business consultant, startup founder, and unapologetic advocate for healing and wholeness, Jaynette is a woman whose life has been a masterclass in resilience. She is a mother, a grandmother, a survivor—and a blueprint for what it means to rebuild, redefine, and reclaim one's life on her own terms.

Born with a fierce spirit and raised with firm love, Jaynette has walked roads many only read about. From pushing a little green wagon through city streets to boardrooms and big dreams, she has consistently chosen purpose over pity and grit over giving up. Her work is rooted in empowering others—especially women—to break cycles, build legacy, and believe again.

Her storytelling is rich with honesty, shaped by experience, and driven by a deep desire to help others see themselves beyond their scars. Whether she's mentoring the next generation of entrepreneurs, advocating for emotional intelligence in leadership, or holding space for healing in her communities, Jaynette brings her whole self—raw, real, and radically loving.

Through this book, she doesn't just give advice—she gives permission: to rise, to rest, to reclaim, and to remember that you are the author of your life. And baby, the pen has always been in your hand.

Preface

I didn't always know I had a voice.

For a long time, I was just trying to survive the noise—the noise of expectations, judgments, trauma, and silence. I was the girl who smiled big and spoke properly, the one who stood out when all I wanted was to fit in. I was the woman who made it look easy, even when it wasn't. And I was the mother who carried a family and dreams on her back while trying to keep her own spirit from breaking.

This book was born in the quiet moments between survival and surrender.

In the hospital at 14, when I didn't want to live anymore, I began the journey of asking hard questions. In boardrooms where I felt unseen, on city buses with my baby in tow, in rooms full of people who misjudged my strength—I began writing this book in my spirit long before I put pen to page.

You Only Need Permission from Yourself is not just a collection of chapters. It is a reclamation.

A reclamation of voice.

A reclamation of identity.

A reclamation of worth.

You don't need to be perfect to begin healing. You don't need to have it all figured out to become whole. You don't need to carry shame for surviving things people will never understand.

You just need permission. And that permission has always been yours to give.

This book is for the woman who's held it down for everyone else and finally wants to hold space for herself. It's for the one who's been strong for so long, she forgot what it felt like to be soft. It's for the daughter, the mother, the friend, the fighter, the visionary, the one who almost gave up—but didn't.

If you've ever felt unseen, unheard, unworthy, or undone—I wrote this for you.

May you find healing in these pages.

May you find yourself.

And most of all, may you finally say yes to you.

With love,

Jaynette M. Lancaster

Contents

Chapter 1
Introduction

"Let your mess become your message."

My life began with laughter and warmth in a loving family, where each day seemed to dawn with promise. But as I journeyed into adulthood and marriage, the scenes of my life drastically shifted. What followed were years fraught with deep depression and reflective challenges, concluding in an essential moment at the tender age of 23.

I intensely recall the day I filed for bankruptcy, a decision born out of desperation and survival. At that time, I was a single parent to my young son, fighting with overwhelming debts and the haunting specter of repossession. The car, essential for my livelihood and my son's stability, was on the brink of being taken away. I had been deceived by false promises, leading to the painful loss that further plunged me into humiliation and despair.

With nowhere else to turn, I found myself drifting, almost homeless, seeking refuge wherever kindness would allow. The weight of my circumstances bore down persistently, overshadowing my attempts to shield my son from the harsh realities unfolding around us.

In the depths of my darkest moments, I was compelled to seek help, finding myself in a psychiatric hospital, grasping for a lifeline amidst the chaos. It was there, among the sterile walls and hushed whispers, that I encountered a compassionate doctor whose words would echo greatly in my soul. She offered a glimmer of hope, reminding me that hardship does not define our ultimate fate and that there were paths forward, even from the depths of misery.

The decision to file for bankruptcy was daunting, yet it became my lifeline, a necessary step toward reclaiming stability and rebuilding shattered dreams. It marked a key turning point, propelling me forward with determination.

Reflecting, I also faced emotional wounds inflicted by those closest to me. My aunt, once a figure of familial support, revealed her true colors through hurtful words and actions, leaving scars that rivaled the pain of financial ruin. It was a reminder of the complexities of human relationships and the betrayals that can sear the heart.

Through it all, I emerged stronger with the hard-earned wisdom that often springs from the deepest wounds. The journey was difficult, fraught with delays and moments of loneliness, yet each problem became a stepping stone toward personal growth and eventual healing.

Today, as I look back on those turbulent chapters of my life, I find comfort in knowing that, while formidable, hardship does not extinguish hope. It is a testament to the human spirit's capacity to endure, to rise above, and to find redemption within the ruins of shattered dreams.

This narrative aims to capture the emotional depth and transformative journey you have found, emphasizing flexibility and the human capacity for revitalization in the face of overwhelming difficulty.

In the middle of these tumultuous events, my mind often wandered back to the preserved memories of my childhood and the warmth of my family. I was fortunate to have been raised in a town that embodied the essence of a melting pot, a place where variety flourished, and community bonds were strong. Our family, expansive and tightly-knit, was a fixture in our small town, known to all either personally or by reputation, especially given my grandfather's status as a successful black man who always prioritized family and community.

My mother's lineage, deeply rooted in this very town, added another layer of familiarity and connection to our surroundings. Despite our challenges, I cherish memories of a generally pleasant upbringing until a crucial moment around the fourth grade.

It was then that I began to experience bed-wetting, a perplexing and distressing development that perplexed my mother. She spared no effort in trying to uncover the cause, setting aside special days just for us and showering me with attention in her quest for answers. However, the root of my distress lay hidden in plain sight within the confines of our own home, where an aunt had taken up residence.

This aunt, once a trusted family member, had transformed into a source of judgment, sneakiness, and verbal abuse. Her critical gaze fell heavily upon me, a chubby child blessed with intellect and wit. In spite of excelling academically and demonstrating maturity beyond my years, I found no support in the safety of my own home during those turbulent times. Instead of the love and nurturing I craved, I encountered confusion and emotional anguish.

The absence of my aunts from my father's side, who had drifted away to tend to their own families, worsened my sense of loneliness. Their departure left a void that was keenly felt, further deepening my isolation.

To compound matters, it later came to light that this same aunt struggled with drug addiction, a revelation that shattered our naivety and reshaped my understanding of the world. The lessons learned about addiction and its devastating impact were seared into my consciousness, imprinting upon me a fierce determination to steer clear of such destructive behaviors and influences.

Yet, despite my resolve, life took an unexpected turn. Driven by a yearning for acceptance and love, I found myself drawn into a relationship that mirrored the chaos and dysfunction I had vowed to avoid. In hindsight, my attraction to someone with a troubled past stemmed from my brokenness, a consequence of years spent in an environment where dysfunction had become normalized.

I shared these painful memories because I was hoping you could learn the resilience that carried me through those dark times, the same resilience that continues to guide me today. Though the scars of the past remain, they serve as my strength and determination to forge a path defined by healing, self-discovery, and, ultimately, a steadfast commitment to breaking the cycle of dysfunction that once threatened to define me.

Growing up in a bustling household of one boy and three girls, our family grew even larger when we welcomed my little brother through adoption during my ninth-grade year. I grew up in our cherished home, which my father meticulously renovated himself, and our early years were infused with fond memories of simpler times. I recall how my mother, reflecting on her own youthful experiences, ensured our upbringing was marked by warmth and togetherness.

However, our family's journey took a turn when, by age eight and a half, we transitioned to a new way of life as Jehovah's Witnesses. This shift meant letting go of traditional celebrations like birthdays and holidays, which inevitably caused some confusion and adjustment at school. Yet, my mother's firm dedication to our understanding and emotional well-being ensured we never felt deprived or left out. She adeptly replaced these familiar festivities with creative gestures that celebrated us in unique ways.

I have fond memories of the transition period when my mom ingeniously crafted a makeshift fireplace in our apartment one Christmas, complete with cookies for Santa and the joyous trimmings of holiday cheer, popcorn strings, and festive decorations—all of which she lovingly arranged to make our home feel magical, just like those we saw on TV.

Post-conversion, she channeled her creativity into new traditions that made every occasion special. Birthdays became mornings of surprises, with beds overflowing with toys to remind us of our worth and celebration. Holidays transformed into lively treasure hunts, where the extended family gathered for grand feasts and playful games, each child distinguished by their unique wrapping paper.

Even in quieter moments, our home remained a hub of activity, with cousins, aunts, uncles, and close family friends always welcomed with open arms. We even shared a beloved dog with our next-door neighbors, a testament to the deep sense of community my parents fostered.

After holiday breaks, returning to school was always a highlight, filled with laughter and games like “Let’s Make a Deal” or “Name That Price,” complete with humorous gag gifts that never failed to elicit smiles. Through it all, my mother’s steadfast commitment to creating joy and unity within our family shone brightly, ensuring that our upbringing was loving and filled with wonder and belonging that shaped us into who we are today.

In our tranquil neighborhood, settled among elderly neighbors who kept watch over us like extended family, our childhood was filled with moments of both abundance and challenge. Our home, a haven brimming with Barbie dolls, Strawberry Shortcake figurines, dollhouses, swimming pools, and miniature cars, was a testament to my mother’s unwavering commitment to ensuring we experienced the joy of childhood to its fullest.

However, amid these treasures were shadows, moments when familial tensions cast a pall over our otherwise idyllic existence. Whether it was an unwelcome family member bringing discord into our midst or spirited scuffles with visiting cousins, these experiences left emotional footprints that remained.

Yet, despite the occasional uproar, I carried within me a dual nature, tender-hearted and nurturing, traits my mother often noted with pride. From a young age, I reveled in caring for others, emulating the nurturing spirit I witnessed in my mother's actions, like bathing my siblings with the same care she gave us.

Our family, viewed from the outside, garnered comparisons to iconic TV families like the Huxtables or the Brady Bunch. Neighbors marveled at our tightly-knit bonds and the structured yet joyful upbringing we received. While other children roamed freely, we found our delight on the porch or within the confines of our home, enveloped in stories and games that nurtured our minds and souls.

Central to our upbringing was my mother's infectious spirit. She was an educator, an advocate, and a devoted parent. She poured her energy into volunteering at schools, fiercely defending us from any hint of academic belittlement. I, too, mirrored her passion for learning, walking at six months and crafting cursive sentences by the tender age of four or five, a testament to the nurturing environment in which she was educated.

Our childhood, marked by both exuberance and trials, was shaped by my mother's boundless love, creativity, and solid commitment to guaranteeing we not only thrived but also cherished every moment, even amidst life's challenges. Her influence remains a guiding light, illuminating the path forward with resilience and a deep appreciation for the beauty found in both simplicity and familial connection.

From a young age, my parents instilled in me values of dignity and aspiration, emphasizing the importance of speaking proper English, carrying oneself with pride, and striving for excellence in all endeavors. These principles, however, set me apart from my peers at school, where conformity often trumped individuality.

I carried the weight of being "chunky" well into my early teens, a factor that, combined with my adherence to my parents' teachings, made me a target for ridicule and exclusion. Even simple decisions, like cutting my hair short in fifth grade to emulate my father, were scorned and misunderstood by classmates who failed to comprehend my family's values.

School became a place of misery, a battleground where my differences marked me as an outsider. I was perceived as indifferent or conceited by my peers, who, in turn, rejected me. The loneliness and rejection grew more pronounced as I entered high school, where the hostility intensified into physical confrontations. Year after year, I faced aggression from girls who sought to provoke me, picking fights and resorting to bullying tactics that tested my resolve.

My mother, recognizing the toll this took on my spirit, urged me to stand up for myself. With her encouragement, I reluctantly embraced confrontation, learning to defend myself amid the turmoil of youth. While this assertiveness earned begrudging respect from some, it further separated me from my peers, particularly Black girls who viewed me with distrust or disdain.

After this turmoil, a deep feeling of unworthiness took root within me. It was compounded by a desperate attempt to end my own life during ninth grade, a cry for help born of despair and isolation. During this darkness, there were glimmers of support, a loyal Filipino friend who stood by my side, and my steadfast boyfriend, whose Jehovah's Witness upbringing posed yet another barrier in my tumultuous journey.

I told a lot about my mother, but my dearest father was no less. My father, a pillar of quiet strength in our family, provided stability and wisdom in contrast to the chaos swirling around me. His few words carried immense weight, offering solace in moments of chaos and uncertainty.

Thus, my teenage years unfolded against a backdrop of internal struggle and external conflict, shaped by a quest for acceptance and understanding that often eluded me. Remember that through the pain and setbacks, you always gleaned lessons in resilience and self-advocacy, navigating a path toward healing and self-acceptance that continues to define yourself and your journey.

I remember how my parents remembered open communication and encouraged us to share our thoughts and feelings freely. Whenever any of us needed a special pick-me-up, they would whisk us away for a day filled with cherished moments and treats, ensuring we felt valued and loved. Our home was not without responsibilities, though; while we were spared mundane chores like dishwashing, making our beds, and tidying our rooms, they were non-negotiables that taught us accountability and discipline.

As a stay-at-home mom, her days were dedicated to nurturing us and imparting life skills that would serve us well into adulthood. Early on, I developed a passion for cooking under her guidance. Whether it was eagerly preparing meals for visiting family or experimenting in the kitchen with my uncle from LA, who graciously indulged my culinary attempts, cooking became both a skill and a source of pride.

Beyond the kitchen, my interest lay in books, whisking me away to fantastical realms where problems seemed manageable and joy was always within reach. Yet, when troubles arose in the real world, I found firm support in my fiercely protective middle sister, who stood as my vocal advocate, ensuring our mother swiftly addressed any challenges we faced.

My youth proved stormy, marked by incidents like having my date stolen at an eighth-grade dance and facing ridicule for my thick glasses, despite my mother's efforts to provide the best for me. Her encouragement, however, propelled me forward. When setbacks occurred, such as not making the cheerleading squad initially, she ardently supported fairness and opportunity, ultimately leading to my successful inclusion on the team the following year.

Throughout high school, I flourished in leadership roles, from cheerleading to basketball and the presidency of the BSU and PEP squads. These achievements were a testament to my mother's belief in nurturing our passions and fostering personal growth beyond mere academics.

Despite the adversity I faced, including being the only Black girl lifeguard and enduring unfounded criticism for enjoying swimming, my mother's belief in embracing life with a smile persisted. The wisdom I harvested from her emphasized that a smile can carry one through even the toughest moments, and this became a guiding principle. Navigating through the tumultuous waters of personal history and the trials of life, I've kept myself on a journey that transcends mere survival. It's a testament to resilience and the power of self-discovery.

For years, I carried the weight of my past like a burden, burying memories deep within the recesses of my mind, hoping they would fade into obscurity. The pain, the rejection, the sense of not belonging, it was indeed a heavy cloak I wore, stifling my voice and my spirit. Yet, through perseverance and the unwavering support of my parents, I found a way to rise above.

Growing up amidst a backdrop of uncertainty and conflicting emotions, I learned early on that resilience is not just about enduring hardships, but it's about finding the strength to rewrite your narrative. My upbringing wasn't conventional; it was marked by moments of isolation and self-doubt, compounded by the harsh realities of emotional and physical abuse in my second marriage. The scars ran deep, threatening to define me indefinitely.

But amidst the darkness, a glimmer of hope emerged. The pivotal moment came when I found my voice again, a voice that had been suppressed for far too long. In reclaiming this voice, I realized the power of my own story, which, while unique to me, echoes with countless others who have faced similar battles.

The decision to write my memoir was not just an exercise in catharsis; it was a declaration of resilience and a light of hope for those who may be navigating their turbulent seas. Through the pages of my book, I invite readers into the inner sanctum of my experiences, where vulnerability meets strength and adversity transforms into empowerment.

I recount the moments of despair and the slow, arduous climb toward healing. It's a narrative of introspection, courage, and determination to break free from the chains of the past. Each chapter is a testament to the human spirit's capacity to endure, evolve, and ultimately thrive.

My story isn't one of victimhood but of victory, a testament to the transformative power of self-belief and resilience. It's a reminder that despite the darkest moments, there is always a path forward, a path illuminated by the unwavering light of hope and the promise of a brighter tomorrow.

As readers journey through my memoir, I hope they come away with optimism and a good understanding of their capacity for resilience. I want them to see that no matter how daunting the obstacles may seem, they have within them the strength to overcome and the courage to forge a life filled with abundance, peace, and fulfillment.

Ultimately, my memoir is a tribute to the human spirit, a celebration of the indomitable will to survive and thrive, no matter the odds. It is evidence of the lasting truth that with perseverance, belief, and the courage to confront our past, we can all find our way to a future defined by hope and possibility.

Chapter 2
Resilient by Choice

There is no doubt that I have faced many things in my life besides the challenges and hardships, but within myself, I found the power of strength and resilience to make significant life changes. At the age of 19 and a half, I made the courageous decision to leave my first husband, driven by a strong feeling that my life needed to be different—for myself and even for my son. I packed my things with determination and a few essentials in a backpack and diaper bag, and I went on a journey while pushing a stroller for what felt like 3 to 5 miles until I reached my aunt's house.

Arriving at my aunt's provided a refuge and a chance to regroup. With no money, clothes, or place to call my own, I relied on her support to decide my next steps. This important moment of my life marked a turning point where I realized my potential to strive for more than the confines of a traditional role. I knew I possessed the drive to achieve and shine beyond the limitations I had previously experienced.

This experience taught me invaluable lessons about independence, resilience, and the power of self-belief. It fueled my determination to create a better future, one where I could pursue my ambitions with strength and purpose. From that moment onward, I accepted a path of growth and empowerment with a vision of a life full of possibility and fulfillment.

Leaving my ex-husband was a decision fraught with challenges, particularly in facing familial and legal obstacles. I was aware that my departure would upset my mother, and my ex-husband and his family were already antagonistic towards me. With few options available, I sought refuge in closets, slept in cars, and relied on the occasional assistance of an old friend who once placed me in a hotel.

During this unrestrained period, my mother's concern intensified to involving the police, putting out notices, and forcing me into hiding with my child. The situation increased with threats of losing custody of my son, fueled by accusations that I was not acting in his best interests. The stress and uncertainty took a toll on my health, which caused me to lose a significant amount of weight within days.

When my parents eventually found me, their shock and disbelief led to unfounded accusations, which included suspicions of drug use. Ultimately, their actions resulted in my son being taken away and placed with his father, an outcome that devastated me extremely.

This experience was deeply distressing and felt like the culmination of a personal crisis. However, it also emphasized my determination to protect myself and my child despite overwhelming odds. It marked a chapter of thoughtful growth and perseverance as I steered through hardship with the conviction that my actions were driven by a commitment to secure a safer and healthier future for my family.

Following those challenging events, I realized the necessity of taming both inner strength and courage while seeking a new support system. To understand the strain it placed on my family, particularly my aunt, I resolved to find alternative resources to avoid further disruption in her life.

Later, at that juncture, I discovered a program designed to assist young women and single mothers in rebuilding their lives. Through this program, I accessed opportunities to stabilize my situation. Then, I secured employment and obtained subsidized housing, which became essential steps in regaining my independence and establishing a stable foundation for myself and my child.

I recognized that many women faced with similar circumstances might struggle to recover or resort to less favorable options such as government assistance or returning to harmful relationships. The emotional abuse and suppression I endured highlighted the critical importance of finding pathways to empowerment and self-sufficiency.

This period of my life was transformative and taught me how to show flexibility in every situation to overcome the misery and trouble in my life. When I seized the resources available and refused to surrender to despair, I rebuilt my life and reclaimed my agency and dignity. It made me grow and affirmed my belief in the potential for positive change despite scary challenges.

Within the tumultuous period of rebuilding my life, I pursued higher education, a goal postponed by earlier challenges. However, my efforts were met with court documents served at school and threatened custody proceedings for my son. This experience left me vulnerable and fearful, contributing to an innate feeling of unworthiness.

During this time, I encountered my next relationship with a man who shared my religious background but had a markedly different perspective on life. This person initially provided strength, protection, and a departure from my previous experiences. Yet, despite these qualities, the relationship proved damaging as I discovered the person's betrayal. He was involved with another woman and ultimately married her.

Throughout these emotional disturbances, the experiences were deeply difficult, but they further helped me shape my journey of self-discovery and resilience.

Each experience taught me valuable lessons about trust, self-worth, and the complexities of relationships. It strengthened my determination to reach a path that prioritizes my well-being and personal growth, free from the confines of past hardships and betrayals.

I remember that I held a variety of jobs, ranging from selling burial plots to working in insurance and administration. Each job was a stepping stone toward achieving stability and providing a better life for myself and my son. I was determined not to conform to societal expectations or be constrained by financial limitations. This drive stemmed from my desire to offer my son the best possible upbringing and prove my provider's capability.

Within the challenges of juggling work and single parenthood, I found comfort and guidance in self-help literature. These books became the foundation of my personal development journey and offered insights and strategies to steer the complexities of life on my own terms. With few friends and a limited social circle, I cherished the bond I formed with a fellow student at school. This new friendship provided much-needed companionship and support during a time when I often felt isolated.

As I reflect on past relationships, I recall a significant gap with my high school friend because of the cultural misunderstandings and my ex-husband's lack of empathy. His refusal to acknowledge and respect Filipino traditions surrounding grief led to a strained relationship that ultimately dissolved. Although reconciliation later occurred, the incident left lasting emotional wounds and underscored the importance of cultural sensitivity and genuine compassion in friendships.

And after that, I also experienced deep isolation within my own family, a feeling that began with my marriage. I felt confined and diminished, as if I had become a possession rather than an individual. The expectations imposed upon me included abandoning my education after completing the 12th grade. Although my parents supported my homeschooling for a semester, I faced resistance when I wanted to return to traditional schooling for the second semester. There was constant friction and resistance, with efforts made to prevent me from pursuing my education.

Obviously, being a young wife and mother, I found myself restricted from typical teenage experiences and social interactions. The pressure to conform to the roles of a wife and caregiver for my son dominated my identity formation during those crucial formative years. The changes demanded of me, from altering my clothing style to conforming to new expectations, were traumatic and disturbing. It took considerable time to recover from the emotional toll of these experiences, which marked the beginning of a period where I felt my inner light dimming.

Moreover, the social changing aspects I encountered then, including anger from peers, worsened my sense of isolation. This was a plain departure from previous challenges I had faced in school. Now, I contended with the deep dissonance of being compelled to embody a persona that felt alien to my true self, all under the guise of love and commitment.

So, if you ever face such difficulties and inconveniences in your life, do not get confused and question your luck and life. Just remember that everything happens for a reason, a reason to experience life's obstacles, as it helps bring about more significant change. It can help you transform and be empowered to forge ahead with strength and determination, and these experiences are fueled by the lessons learned along the way. Believe me, it's a blessing to be on your own.

Women often stay in relationships or marriages due to external perceptions and societal pressures. The fear of judgment from others can weigh heavily and compel them to maintain appearances and wear a facade of strength and resilience like a superhero's cape. This facade preserves their courage and fortitude and enables them to face challenging circumstances.

However, women who defy societal norms and choose to leave relationships or challenge cultural expectations often face ostracism and criticism. In many cultures, such decisions are met with disapproval and disdain, leading to social exclusion and emotional hardship. This societal rejection can be very damaging and can cause emotional distress and isolation that undermines self-esteem and well-being.

In my own experience, changing my marital status in the religious organization I'm part of resulted in nearly three decades of gossip, discussions, and negative perceptions within our community. The repercussions were deeply hurtful and uncomfortable, creating an environment that could easily crush one's spirit and leave them feeling ostracized and unworthy.

Such challenges require immense strength and flexibility as they demand the courage to confront societal expectations and judgments while reclaiming one's identity and pursuing personal fulfillment. Besides, many women find within themselves the resilience to persevere, redefine their paths, and promote empowerment beyond societal confines.

Nevertheless, I chose to persevere, maintain a positive outlook, and remind myself that my worth is affirmed by a higher power regardless of others' opinions. I understood that people, despite their religious or spiritual affiliations, may still harbor unchanged attitudes, lack emotional maturity, or project their own issues onto others. Some individuals may turn to religion to cope with personal insecurities or struggles, inadvertently projecting their challenges onto those around them.

I faced significant challenges within my congregation when I refused to submit to the demands and demeaning behavior of certain individuals, primarily men who wanted to exert authority over me, contrary to my beliefs and convictions. This resistance resulted in unjust accusations and even a certified letter labeled me as a disruptor of the congregation's purity.

But I maintained my resolve to stand firm in my beliefs and assert my dignity. I refused to be coerced into conforming to unjust practices or subjugating myself to undue authority. This experience highlighted the importance of staying true to oneself and resolving difficult circumstances with grace and integrity.

If your faith remains a source of strength and solace, guides you through adversity, and reinforces your belief in a higher purpose beyond human judgments, hold onto it and don't let go. It can teach you resilience and the importance of remaining steadfast in the face of adversity, trusting in your convictions, and recognizing that true spiritual growth comes from authenticity and integrity rather than conformity to societal or religious expectations, especially for women.

Women should confront challenges promptly by avoiding suppression of their feelings or remaining silent out of fear of being perceived as disrespectful or distasteful. It's crucial for them to assert themselves and recognize that the hardships they face and others' projections do not define their worth. Understanding that difficulties and pain are temporary but can provide perspective, alongside the knowledge that there are resources available today, such as support groups and counseling, that offer opportunities to discover one's purpose or explore new paths.

Resilience is a key attribute to encourage, but it is equally important for women to acknowledge that they do not always have to embody the stereotype of a forever-strong woman, especially if it leads to toxicity or harm to their well-being. Embracing vulnerability and asking for support are vital aspects of healing. It is empowering to realize that strength can be found in various forms and situations and that seeking help when needed is a sign of strength.

By accepting these principles, women can face challenges with greater confidence by knowing they can adapt, grow, and ultimately thrive, not just suffer hardship. They can build resilience while honoring their needs for support and self-care, fostering a balanced approach to facing life's obstacles.

I remember how I had set aside aspirations such as modeling gigs and pageants that I deeply cherished and had been passionate about before becoming pregnant and getting married. These opportunities seemed to vanish, yet it is essential for women to remember that they can always revisit their dreams. Whether returning to those pursuits in their original form or exploring new avenues, it is never too late to reignite that spark of personal growth and fulfillment.

If you feel adrift or unsure of how to proceed, your own stories can serve as a blueprint for resilience and renewal. By embracing your experiences thus far, you can draw strength from them and use them as a foundation to rebuild and pursue your passions. Each path may vary in direction or method, but the essence of reclaiming one's aspirations remains steadfast—a testament to your ability to adapt and thrive despite setbacks.

Ultimately, the journey back to pursuing our dreams is a personal one with determination and a willingness to evolve.

It is about recognizing that delays do not define us and that we can rediscover and pursue the aspirations that bring us fulfillment and joy with perseverance and self-belief. As we honor our journey and remain open to new possibilities, we empower ourselves to reclaim our light and forge a path toward renewed purpose and achievement.

Chapter 3
You Are Strong

Being challenged in life is inevitable. Being defeated is Optional.

— Roger Crawford

As I reflect on my experience from seventh grade, I realize that trouble seems to be an unavoidable part of life, no matter how much we try to avoid it despite our best efforts to go about life. I was a pretty average kid who found myself in a situation where trouble came knocking unexpectedly. I was this awkward, emotional kid back then, just trying to fit in and do well in school. I wore glasses and was in leadership roles, which was a bit different from what most people might expect.

My popularity came from having boy cousins who cheered me on and pushed me into the spotlight, which was a blessing and a challenge as well. I always tried to be kind and loving, but trouble found me instead. I remember my very first fight vividly. I was entirely caught off guard by a girl who decided she wanted to fight me for reasons I couldn't understand. I had done nothing to provoke this, but it didn't matter. She had a big following, and everyone was egging her on. I was terrified, not just of the physical confrontation, but of the humiliation and the repercussions at home. I was afraid that my skirt might fly up and expose my underwear, which added to my anxiety.

In that moment, I had to call together every ounce of bravery. I knew I had to stand up for myself, even though it was the last thing I wanted to do. I fought back, and to my surprise, I managed to hold my own and even come out on top. But the fear of the consequences at home loomed large. My family had always taught me to defend myself and avoid trouble whenever possible. It was a confusing and stressful situation, and I didn't know how to explain it all, so I called my grandmother to pick me up from school.

Looking back, I realize that trouble is inevitable. Even when we strive to be kind and avoid conflict, we can still find ourselves in difficult situations. What matters is how we handle those moments, see the strength within ourselves to face them, and guide the aftermath. My experience taught me that trouble can come from unexpected places and people and that sometimes, all we can do is face it head-on and hope for the best.

Losing my aunt was a severe and heart-wrenching experience. She was the one who stood by me during one of the most challenging times in my life when I wanted to leave my husband, feeling vulnerable, penniless, and unsure of anything in life. Her support was like peace in the storm, and she guided me through uncertainty and fear. When she passed away, it felt as though a part of me had been ripped away, leaving an emptiness that was hard to fill. The grief was so overwhelming that it felt like my heart had been ripped out of my chest and led me to steer life with loss and isolation.

During that time, I also didn't have my son with me, which compounded the feelings of loneliness and despair. It was as though I was floating through a dark and stormy sea without a compass and wrestling with my aunt's absence and my child's absence.

The weight of these losses was almost too much to bear, and I often felt like I was standing at the edge of an emotional chasm. Yet, in the depths of this grave sorrow, I learned an invaluable lesson about staying strong when things get tough. Strength isn't just about physical strength or pushing through difficulties; it's also about finding the inner grit to keep going even when everything seems to be falling apart.

In my darkest moments, I realized that staying strong meant allowing myself to grieve, feel the pain, and acknowledge the depth of my loss. It meant reaching out for support from friends, family, or professional counselors and not being afraid to lean on others when I needed it most. Staying strong also involved finding small ways to cope with the overwhelming emotions. It was about permitting myself to take one day at a time, to focus on the small victories and moments of clarity that could help me move forward. It meant recognizing that it was okay not to be alright and that healing is a gradual process that doesn't follow a strict timeline.

Even when everything felt uncertain and overwhelming, I learned that strength could be found in living, hoping, and finding moments of peace in the chaos. It was about adoring the memories of my aunt and holding onto the love and support she had given me. Her memory became a source of strength, reminding me that even in the face of profound loss, there is a way to find hope and strength.

In essence, staying strong through tough times is not about being unaffected by pain or loss but about finding the courage to face it and to keep moving forward, step by step.

It's about welcoming the support around us and allowing ourselves the grace to heal while holding onto the love and lessons our loved ones have given us. If you steer through life without the support of family, dealing with strained relationships can be incredibly challenging, but there are ways to stay strong through these trials. First and foremost, it's important to acknowledge and accept your emotions and allow yourself to feel and process the hurt, anger, or sadness that comes with a lack of familial support.

To build your own support system, it is crucial to seek out friends, mentors, or support groups who can provide the encouragement and understanding that you might not get from your family.

Also, it is important to prioritize self-care, such as maintaining a healthy lifestyle and engaging in activities that bring you joy, help you manage stress, and support your well-being. Set realistic goals, recognize your strengths that can boost your motivation and self-esteem, and remind you of your ability to overcome challenges. Suppose interactions with family members become too painful. In that case, setting boundaries to protect your emotional health is necessary, as well as seeking professional help from a therapist or counselor who can offer strategies and a safe space to explore your feelings.

If you want to counteract feelings of responsibility or guilt while adopting personal growth through hardship, provide yourself a purpose, then focus on the positive aspects of your life and practice self-compassion. You can help yourself find joy in small moments, whether through hobbies or time spent with your children or loved ones, which can offer comfort and a deception of normality. By incorporating these small strategies, you can continue to drive your challenges with empowerment and hope. I cried often. But after facing many difficulties, I realized those experiences always had a way of making me stronger—even when the moments felt overwhelming.

Each difficulty has pushed me beyond my comfort zone and taught me valuable lessons about myself and life. Looking back at the most challenging times, I can see how they have shaped me into a more inventive and resourceful person.

One major lesson I've learned is the importance of adaptability. Challenges often force me to think on my feet and develop creative solutions I wouldn't have considered otherwise. For example, when I was juggling multiple jobs and raising my son alone, I had to learn how to manage my time effectively and prioritize my responsibilities.

This experience taught me that I am more capable than I initially believed and that I can handle more than I thought possible.

Another lesson is the value of perseverance. It's easy to feel like giving up is the only option during tough times. However, sticking with it, even when it feels like progress is slow, has shown me perseverance, which can lead to unexpected rewards.

Each small step forward, no matter how insignificant it may seem, contributes to overcoming the more significant challenges and helps me persevere through difficult times. I've developed several strategies.

First, I focus on setting small, achievable goals. Breaking down a big challenge into smaller, manageable tasks makes it feel less daunting and helps me maintain momentum. I also remind myself to take breaks and practice self-care. It's essential to recharge and avoid burnout, which means taking time for activities that bring me joy and relaxation.

Another tip is to acquire a positive mindset. I try to reframe challenges as opportunities for growth rather than insurmountable barriers.

This shift in perspective can make it easier to stay motivated and see the value in the struggle. Additionally, I lean on my support network, even if it's just a few friends, sometimes even a stranger who became a friend, or mentors.

Their encouragement and perspective can be a source of strength when I feel overwhelmed. Lastly, I keep a journal to track my progress and reflect on my experiences. Writing down my thoughts and feelings helps me process my emotions and recognize how far I've come. It also provides a record of past challenges and how I overcame them, which can be reassuring when facing new difficulties.

So always remember that while challenges can be incredibly tough, they also offer opportunities for growth and learning. By adopting these strategies and focusing on the lessons learned, I can overcome difficulties with greater strength and become more assertive on the other side.

Chapter 4
Positive Mindset

My life has been far from easy, but I've learned an invaluable lesson: the power of a positive mindset. Negativity can be destructive, leading to anxiety, depression, and poor decision-making. It can strain relationships and impact physical health. It can even create a self-fulfilling prophecy, where negative expectations lead to negative outcomes.

In contrast, a positive mindset can transform our experiences. It shifts our focus from limitations to possibilities, from problems to opportunities for growth. This doesn't mean ignoring challenges but facing them with resilience and optimism. Reflecting on my journey, I realize that despite numerous setbacks since I was 17, I've always had to push forward. There's no going back, and this forward momentum has propelled me through countless obstacles. There have been times I felt overwhelmed, but the responsibility to persevere always rested with me.

The path to positivity involves daily practice. It means consciously choosing optimism, even when faced with adversity. It means reframing challenges as opportunities for growth. Additionally, negativity narrows one's perspective, limiting the ability to recognize opportunities or appreciate achievements. Ultimately, a negative mindset can lead to inactivity and prevent personal and professional advancement. To address this mindset, you need to encourage self-awareness and practice positive thinking techniques to manage a more balanced and optimistic outlook.

The power of positivity is transformative. It offers a powerful counter to our challenges and hardships. Maintaining a positive mindset can significantly alter our experiences by focusing on possibilities rather than limitations.

When we view problems as opportunities for growth, we harness a force that propels us forward, even in the face of difficulties. Reflecting on my journey, I realize that even with the struggles I've faced since I was 17, it's important to focus on moving forward rather than dwelling on past hardships. As the saying goes, "It is useless to cry over spilled milk." Life has often pushed me to advance because retreating isn't an option. When there is no way to go back, the only choice is to press on.

A positive mindset enables us to navigate difficulties with greater ease. It fosters resilience, creativity, and motivation, even when progress is slow. It allows us to bounce back from setbacks and explore alternative solutions. It's about more than just positive thinking; it's about cultivating a lifestyle that supports optimism and growth.

I've learned that true progress often comes from confronting challenges head-on. While the urge to retreat can be strong, it's in facing adversity that we discover our inner strength.

Those moments when I felt lost and disheartened were also the moments that taught me the most about resilience. The journey toward positivity is ongoing. It requires daily effort and commitment to becoming the best version of ourselves. By focusing on these efforts, we can develop the strength to transform hardships into opportunities. Positivity empowers us to navigate life's complexities with optimism and grace. Through positive thinking and self-care, we can continuously move forward, turning challenges into catalysts for self-improvement.

If you want to practice positivity, focus on daily efforts to nurture a positive mindset. Whenever you face trouble or are confused about what to do next, embrace a positive mindset. It helps you overcome difficulties and empowers you to thrive, grow, and transform problems into opportunities. The power of positivity is truly transformative and can be a crucial antidote to the challenges and difficulties we face in life. Adopting a positive mindset doesn't merely change your viewpoint but also reshapes your experiences and outcomes. When we focus on opportunities rather than problems, we tap into a force that helps us handle difficulties with greater ease and resilience. The key to progress lies in forward momentum. Even when it feels like moving backward is the only option, facing challenges head-on is essential for advancement.

The idea of moving forward has become a guiding principle in my life, pushing me through numerous hurdles. In moments of intense struggle, when I felt like I was falling apart, the challenge of standing up and moving forward was mine alone to face. Those periods of feeling lost and disheartened were deeply trying, but also highlighted that the strength to rise from hardship comes from within. When I hesitated and found myself at a low point, I always found the inner resolve to push through, which was essential to overcoming those challenges. The journey toward positivity involves more than just acknowledging these truths; it requires daily practice and commitment to become the best version of ourselves. By focusing on these daily efforts, you can build the strength to transform hardships into opportunities for growth.

Ultimately, understanding and practicing positivity helps you navigate life's complexities with greater strength and optimism. Through positive thinking and self-care practices, you can continually move forward and turn challenges into opportunities for self-improvement. A positive mindset is a powerful tool for changing how we perceive and address challenges.

Approaching difficulties with optimism allows us to bounce back from delays and opens us to creative solutions and alternative approaches. It also boosts motivation and energy levels, driving us to stay engaged even when progress seems slow.

Chapter 5
The Business Woman

In business, balancing competency, leadership, and being personable is crucial. While some aspects of business are straightforward, many situations are complex and nuanced. Therefore, it's essential to understand both the technical and human elements of running a business.

You need a solid grasp of business principles and practices, such as accounting, operations, and hiring. Simply having a business idea isn't enough; you must educate yourself and be prepared to make informed decisions, even difficult ones. For instance, when it comes to terminating employees, handling the situation with care is crucial. Over time, I learned to manage these tough conversations respectfully, making the process smooth. Even in challenging situations, treating people with dignity can lead to positive outcomes and continued professional relationships.

A lot of people underestimate women in business, partly because society has set certain expectations. However, I learned valuable lessons from my first boss and his wife, who ran a family-owned business. Even though the wife wasn't heavily involved in the daily operations, she understood every aspect of the business.

Here's what they taught me, and this advice has been essential in building a successful business and a positive work environment:

- Be in the habit of sharing knowledge, and always give out free information if you have it, even if you didn't get it for free yourself. Helping others can be valuable.
- Always pay yourself, and make sure you pay yourself for your work. It's important for your financial well-being.
- Always understand your business before starting it; thoroughly understand all the laws, rules, and aspects related to it. It's not just a hobby; it requires serious planning and knowledge.
- Be aware of what others in your industry are doing, and know your competition.
- Always remember there's more than one way to do something and that someone else may be smarter or more experienced than you. Having a team member who knows more than you can be incredibly beneficial. Learn from each other.
- Even if you're the CEO, understand and be willing to do the basic tasks that keep the business running. This shows your employees that you value every part of the business and helps you understand their roles better.

My first boss was amazing. He let me work in different roles within the company and always encouraged me to learn and grow. He wanted me to find ways to ensure a good life for me and my son. One of the best pieces of advice he gave me was, "Everyone deserves the finer things in life. Make sure you experience them so you can aspire to have them." This advice was powerful.

When you see or experience something better, it changes your mindset. You start to believe you deserve it and can achieve it.

This same boss would bring me the salary rosters from his father's team, the Golden State Warriors, and joke that I should date guys like those. During a tough breakup, he and his team were incredibly supportive. Instead of being strict, they offered me other opportunities and allowed me time off for modeling gigs. They even helped me get a chance to work with the Raiders and other exciting projects.

Being surrounded by such supportive and inspiring people early on helped me learn to be an entrepreneur. They showed me that the people you surround yourself with can greatly influence you. If you're around uplifting and ambitious people, it pushes you to grow and succeed. Eventually, I worked for the NFL's Oakland Raiders for 11 years.

In today's world, Black women, in particular, face a lot of disrespect and are often placed at the bottom of the social hierarchy. This issue is part of a larger problem where women, in general, are not respected or recognized for their full potential. Many people wrongly believe that women are too emotional or incapable of leading, but many examples prove otherwise.

Right now, women outnumber men globally, which makes it an especially important time to highlight female leadership. It's crucial to show young girls that they, too, can achieve great things and have the opportunity to make a significant impact in the world. Women bring compassion and emotional intelligence to leadership roles. They are not seeking to overshadow men but to work alongside them. Women aim to demonstrate that they are just as capable, intelligent, and valuable as men in shaping the world.

There are many famous female leaders, but I will discuss three who have made great impacts across various fields and demonstrated the strength, intelligence, and vision women bring to leadership roles: Marian Wright Edelman, the first African American woman admitted to the Mississippi Bar, was known for founding the Children's Defense Fund in 1973 to advocate for poor children, children of color, and children with disabilities; Kamala Harris made history as the first female, Black, and South Asian Vice President of the United States, focusing on issues like criminal justice reform and consumer protection; and Malala Yousafzai, a Nobel Peace Prize laureate, became a global advocate for girls' education following her survival of a Taliban assassination attempt.

These women have broken barriers and set new standards for leadership, demonstrating how diverse perspectives can drive meaningful change and progress in various sectors.

As a woman, if they can, then why can't you?

My mother always emphasized that education is crucial and the key to success. I took her advice to heart and pushed myself hard to seize every opportunity. Even though I didn't have a degree, I excelled by showing up fully prepared and performing at my best. I did whatever it took to stand out, stay updated on industry trends, and maintain a strong vocabulary. I was driven by a personal challenge to prove myself and show that I could hold higher positions, like Director of HR or Chief Operations Officer. I was willing to accept lower salaries or lesser titles if it meant moving closer to my goals because I knew I was capable and smarter than many others in those roles. There was a time when a woman was hired for a position that I felt should have been mine, and she admitted that she didn't know how to do the job and relied on others for that.

It was frustrating because it seemed like the company chose her based on her appearance or ethnicity rather than her skills. Sometimes, it feels unfair when we, who have worked hard and gained experience, see others with less knowledge or experience being chosen for roles. It makes me wonder if I would have the position I deserve if I had a degree, despite my experience and capabilities.

As a Black woman, I've worked hard to listen to advice, educate myself, and earn the licenses and certificates needed to be where I deserve to be. It's not just Black women who face challenges without a degree; Black men and many others do, too. But with effort, discipline, and self-development, you can overcome these challenges.

Despite hardships or negativity, focusing on your goals and intentions is important. I've experienced working in companies that felt like family, and my first company, in particular, gave me and my son opportunities I wouldn't have had otherwise. I appreciated their support and how they treated me respectfully, even when dealing with difficult clients. One time, a client was disrespectful when he saw I was a Black woman, but the company stood up for me and made it clear that such behavior would not be tolerated.

This supportive environment helped me a lot, although it didn't directly help me start my own business. However, I received valuable guidance on where to go and what to do, which was like having a mentor.

Chapter 6
Mental Health

Mental health is as important as physical health, yet we often overlook it as we go about our lives. We put so much emphasis on physical fitness, our appearance, and overall well-being, but rarely pause to think about the state of our mind.

Just as we commit to eating healthy, staying active, and keeping ourselves well-groomed, our mental health requires similar dedication and care. Imagine navigating life without tending to your mind—it's like walking into a downpour without any protection, fully exposed to the elements. How can you expect to stay unaffected? Your mental well-being forms the basis of how you experience and interact with the world, and it must get the attention it needs.

If you had a physical injury, you'd never leave it untreated. When you're feeling unwell, you won't hesitate to seek medical help. So why do we delay or shy away from addressing emotional pain? Our mental health should be approached with the same urgency and care as our physical health. As Socrates wisely put it, "The unexamined life is not worth living." It's a powerful reminder that nurturing our mental state is essential for leading a balanced and meaningful life.

Unfortunately, I had to learn this lesson the hard way.

When I was 17, my life took a sharp and unexpected turn. I found myself in a psychiatric hospital—not because I chose to be there, but because I was forced. I didn't have a say in the matter. The experience left deep scars, some visible, but most of them buried within. Looking back now, I can see that I desperately needed help, but at the time, I felt nothing but fear and entrapment.

My life was in complete disarray. I was still so young, trying to juggle the overwhelming responsibilities of being a mother and wife while barely out of my teenage years. Not long before, I had been a high school cheerleader with big dreams and a life full of possibilities ahead of me. But those dreams quickly faded, replaced with the harsh reality of trying to survive adulthood, marriage, and motherhood all at once.

Then came the day that everything changed. It started like any other morning. I was getting ready to head out for work, thinking it would be a routine day. But as we drove to the public transportation stop, my husband and I had a heated argument. He was adamant that I shouldn't be working and that my role was to stay home, take care of our child, and manage our household.

His words left me feeling suffocated, as if my identity and independence were slipping away. Then, in a moment of cruelty, he left me stranded. I was half-dressed in a part of town I didn't know, confused, and scared.

In that moment of desperation, a stranger approached me. She saw the distress in my eyes and asked what had happened. I could barely form words between my tears, but she didn't need an explanation.

Without judgment, she took me to her home, offering me shelter and kindness at a time when I felt completely abandoned. It was a small act, but it meant the world to me. Her compassion pulled me from the edge of despair and gave me the strength to keep moving forward.

When I finally made it back home, I wasn't met with comfort or understanding. Instead, I walked into a room full of my family: my mother, aunt, husband, and in-laws. They had already made up their minds about what was best for me. I was to be admitted to the hospital, and my opinion didn't matter. It was as if my voice had been erased from my own life. They believed something was wrong with me, and their solution was to take control.

Once admitted to the hospital, I was thrown into an environment that terrified me. I had never seen anything like it before. People around me bore visible signs of their inner pain—scars from self-harm, bruises, and hollow eyes that told stories of battles fought silently.

I was surrounded by individuals who had attempted suicide, who harmed themselves, and who wore their pain like a second skin. It was a dark, unfamiliar world, and I felt both isolated and overwhelmed.

I had never been exposed to such raw suffering before. Witnessing it shook me to my core. I learned about self-harm, about the darkness that drives people to hurt themselves when the emotional pain becomes too unbearable. It was a reality I had been blind to until then, and it forced me to reflect on my own neglect of my mental health.

The days in the hospital were terrifying, but they also changed me in ways I didn't expect. Group therapy sessions were filled with stories of unimaginable struggle. I listened to people share their darkest moments, their heartbreak, and their battles with mental illness.

It made me realize just how much pain can be hidden beneath the surface. Many of these people had stories that broke my heart, and it taught me an important lesson: you never honestly know what someone else is going through.

That experience shifted my perspective on life. It made me approach others more empathetically and understanding because I had seen firsthand how invisible pain can be. It showed me the importance of kindness, even to strangers. Sometimes, the smallest acts of compassion can make the most significant difference to someone who feels lost.

In those early days, I kept quiet. I thought if I stayed silent long enough, if I didn't engage, they might let me leave. I convinced myself that if I ignored everything around me, I could avoid dealing with what was really happening. But that's not how it works with mental health.

You can't simply pretend it doesn't exist and hope it disappears. After two weeks of saying almost nothing, one of the doctors took me aside. She told me that unless I started participating in my own recovery, I could be there much longer than I ever expected. That shook me to my core. The fear of being stuck in that place, with no end in sight, scared me far more than anything else.

It was at that moment that I realized I had no choice but to speak up, to find my voice again. At first, the words came slowly, almost unwillingly. I had spent so long keeping my feelings locked away that it felt foreign to express them. But little by little, I started to open up. I began to talk about my emotions, about the weight I had been carrying in silence for so long. It wasn't easy. In fact, it was one of the hardest things I'd ever done. But I knew that if I didn't, I would never make it out of that hospital.

As I started speaking, I began to feel a shift within me. The act of expressing my pain, my fears, and my struggles was liberating. Slowly, I felt the fog begin to lift. I was told I could go home within a week of opening up. That was the first time in a long while that I felt like I was gaining some control over my life again.

During my stay, they put me on medication, something they said would help me manage my emotions. I had hoped it would make a difference, but it did the opposite. The medication seemed to trigger something awful in me—terrifying side effects that made me feel as though my mind and body were no longer my own. At times, it felt like my head was going to explode. I couldn't think clearly, and my body felt like it was rebelling against me. Far from being the solution, the medication became another problem.

It was a harsh lesson. I had always believed that doctors knew best, that their prescribed treatments would automatically work. But that's not always the case. The medication that was meant to help me was doing more harm than good, and it made me realize something crucial: not all treatments are right for everyone. What works for one person may not work for another, and it's essential to trust your own experience when something feels wrong.

Looking back, I wish I had spoken up sooner about the side effects I was experiencing. But I learned from that experience that advocating for yourself is okay. If a treatment isn't working for you—whether it's medication, therapy, or anything else—it's vital to speak out. You have the right to question what's being prescribed and to seek alternatives if necessary. Your mental and physical health is in your hands, and you should always trust your instincts when something feels off.

"Our greatest glory is not in never falling, but in rising every time we fall"

— Confucius.

You have to rise, even when the way forward is unclear, and the path to healing seems distant. This truth became all too real during my time in the psychiatric hospital. Group therapy and one-on-one sessions were a core part of my experience, even though they challenged me in ways I wasn't prepared for. Initially, group therapy was daunting. I sat in a room full of strangers, listening to stories of pain and loss that seemed far more tragic than mine.

Their struggles were raw, and their emotions were laid bare for all to witness. It felt overwhelming, but as time passed, I came to understand one simple truth: we all carry our own burdens. No one was judging me for my struggles, just as I wasn't judging them for theirs. We were all in that room for the same reason—because life had knocked us down, and we were trying to find a way back to our feet.

But while group therapy helped me see that I wasn't alone, individual therapy was a different challenge. I never felt entirely comfortable with the therapist I was assigned, and that made it difficult for me to open up. I tried, but there was always this wall between us. Over time, I learned an important lesson: not every therapist is a good fit for every person, and that's okay. Therapy should feel like a safe space, and it's crucial to find someone you connect with, someone who understands you in a way that makes healing possible.

It took me a while to realize that seeking help wasn't a sign of weakness but courage.

As Mariska Hargitay once said, ***"Healing takes time, and asking for help is a courageous step."***

Therapy can be a powerful tool in the journey toward healing, but finding the right therapist and the right guide is just as important as the process itself.

For me, therapy had an additional layer of complexity. As a Black woman, there's often a cultural stigma around seeking mental health care. In many communities, therapy is seen as something reserved for those who are "crazy" or "certifiably ill." It's not openly talked about or encouraged. I didn't discuss my therapy with my family for fear of being judged or labeled as weak. This stigma made an already isolating experience feel even lonelier. The reality is that mental health struggles are real, but in many communities, seeking professional help is still seen as taboo. These barriers need to be broken down so we can normalize taking care of our minds as much as our bodies.

After being discharged from the hospital, I was fortunate enough to meet a group of doctors who helped me see things more clearly. They made me realize that for years, I had been controlled by my mother, by my circumstances, and by my own fears. That realization was hard to swallow, but it was the first step toward reclaiming my life. They helped me understand that, despite everything, I still had a say in how my life would unfold. But that meant I had to stop staying silent. For too long, I had allowed others to dictate my choices and was too afraid to challenge them. But I learned the hard way that silence is not a solution. I had to find my voice, speak up for myself, and take ownership of my life. It wasn't an easy journey, but it was a necessary one.

Maggie Kuhn once said, ***"Speak your mind, even if your voice shakes."***

Speaking up isn't just about being heard; it's about reclaiming your power. It's about recognizing that your thoughts, your feelings, and your experiences are valid. It's about standing tall, even when you're scared, and knowing that your voice matters.

Two years after my hospitalization, I faced one of the most difficult choices of my life: I left my husband. It was a decision I knew in my heart was necessary, but it wasn't one that many people around me supported. To them, I was walking away from stability, from the familiar. But I was walking toward freedom—something I had never honestly had before. I didn't have much when I left—no car, no savings, and no place to call my own. But I had something far more valuable: my independence. And that was priceless.

Leaving meant stepping into the unknown. It was terrifying. I had never entirely relied on myself before, and suddenly, I was responsible for everything. The fear was real, but so was the exhilaration of finally making choices for me, not for anyone else. It felt like I was finally living life on my terms. But that newfound freedom came with its own set of challenges. I stumbled and made mistakes, and there were moments when I questioned whether I had the strength to keep going.

When you're in survival mode, it's easy to lose sight of who you are. You start making decisions out of desperation rather than clarity, which can lead you down dark paths. I found myself surrounded by people who took advantage of my vulnerability. I attracted individuals—both friends and romantic partners—who saw my insecurities and used them against me. It was a brutal lesson, but I had to learn how to protect myself.

I realized that being strong wasn't just about enduring hardship; it was about standing up for myself, setting boundaries, and walking away from people without my best interests.

As Tony Gaskins wisely said, "You teach people how to treat you by what you allow, what you stop, and what you reinforce." I had to internalize that truth. It wasn't easy, but it was essential to my growth. I had spent so long allowing others to dictate how I should live, what I should accept, and who I should be. Breaking free from that mindset was painful, but it was the only way I could start to heal.

Mental health, I've come to understand, is not a one-time fix. It's not a destination you arrive at fully healed and never struggling again. It's an ongoing journey that requires constant care, just like physical health. There will always be setbacks, moments when old wounds resurface, or new challenges arise. But those struggles don't mean you're failing. They're part of the process.

If you're in a place where you feel overwhelmed, where the weight of your mental health is crushing you, remember that you are not alone. There is help available, whether it comes from therapy, medication, support groups, or simply opening up to a trusted friend.

Sometimes, all it takes is one conversation to start shifting the tides. You have to prioritize your mind because it's your most powerful tool. Without mental clarity and peace, every other part of your life suffers.

Albert Einstein once said, "Insanity is doing the same thing over and over again and expecting different results."

That quote hit home for me because I lived in a cycle of repeating the same mistakes for so long, hoping for change that never came. If you want to heal, you have to break that cycle. You must be brave enough to do something different, speak up, and make decisions that scare you but will ultimately set you free.

Taking control of your life isn't easy. It's messy, it's uncomfortable, and at times it feels overwhelming.

But it's necessary if you want to live rather than survive truly. Healing doesn't come without effort, but the rewards are worth every step you take. You're stronger than you know, and the power to change your life lies within you.

It took me years to understand that speaking up, standing tall, and demanding better for myself wasn't selfish but survival. It was reclaiming my narrative and refusing to let anyone else write it for me. And that's a lesson I hope everyone who reads this can take to heart: your story is yours to tell. Don't let anyone else hold the pen.

If you're struggling, know this—you can do more than you think.

The journey to healing is long and sometimes exhausting, but each step forward brings you closer to the person you're meant to be.

You have the strength to change, to grow, and to rise above whatever is holding you back. Believe in that strength, and never stop fighting for the life you deserve.

Chapter 7
Careful Who You Date

Relationships can be one of the most rewarding aspects of life, but they can also bring some of the deepest challenges, especially when your partner has a history of drug and alcohol addiction. My experience with this started innocently enough, but it turned into something much more complex and painful than I could have ever anticipated.

When I first met him, he had been clean and sober for six years. He was confident, charming, and seemingly stable. I thought I had met someone who had overcome his past and was ready for a fresh start.

I believed that with the right amount of understanding, knowledge, and patience, I could walk beside him through anything life threw our way. I even went as far as immersing myself in the culture of recovery, learning about Narcotics Anonymous (NA) and Alcoholics Anonymous (AA). I thought that by equipping myself with knowledge about addiction, I would be prepared for anything. But no amount of reading can fully prepare you for the reality of living with someone who has fought—and is still fighting—those battles.

What I learned in the following months was that being in a relationship with a recovering addict often brings a lot of hidden trauma, insecurities, and issues that can resurface unexpectedly. No matter how long someone has been clean, the scars of addiction can linger. And these scars aren't always visible at first glance.

At the beginning, he was magnetic. He was the kind of person who could walk into any room and command attention. He was loud, flamboyant, and always had a story to tell. He was well-known in our community, the kind of guy who had been a high school football star, and his presence still carried that same energy.

Everywhere we went, someone knew him; someone would come up to shake his hand, and someone would talk about the "good old days." It was impressive, and in the beginning, I saw it as a strength. He was sociable, well-liked, and confident. I thought his ability to connect with people would complement my quieter nature.

But what I didn't see right away was how that loud confidence often masked deeper insecurities. He always needed attention. It was like he thrived on validation from others and couldn't be left alone with his thoughts. My business partner at the time noticed how much of my energy was being consumed by him and warned me, suggesting that maybe I needed to step back a little. But I ignored the warning signs.

My family had always warned me about dating someone with a history of addiction. They were cautious, perhaps overly so, but I hid the truth from them. I didn't want them to know about his past, thinking that it wasn't relevant anymore since he had been clean for six years.

I convinced myself that people could change and that love could conquer anything. But I wasn't prepared for the emotional toll that came with loving someone who had battled those demons.

At the time, I thought I was strong enough to handle anything. I had faced my own challenges, so I believed that helping someone else face theirs wouldn't be much different. But addiction is tricky. It doesn't just affect the person battling it; it affects everyone around them, even if the addiction itself seems to be in the past.

Everything seemed fine in the beginning. We met at a business networking event, and how things aligned was almost too perfect. He needed help refinancing his house, and I was in a position to help. I saw his financials, and everything seemed legitimate. He was successful, or at least appeared to be. He told me about his past upfront—about his history with drugs and alcohol, how he had turned his life around, and how committed he was to staying clean.

I respected that honesty and thought that if he could be open about something so complex, he could be open about anything. I soon realized I was wrong.

A few months into the relationship, I found a bag of pills hidden in our closet. He was sneaky and often lied, and it became clear that he wasn't as transparent as I had thought. He would disappear for long periods and later confess that he had been cheating, but the lies were so intricate that I found it hard to untangle the truth. His loud, confident persona began to feel like a mask that he used to cover his insecurities and dishonesty.

One day, a woman called me. She was furious, saying he had been seeing her the entire time he was with me. She claimed they had been together for years, and I didn't know what to believe. When I confronted him, he denied everything, and in my confusion and hurt, I chose to believe him. I dismissed her as crazy, thinking she was just trying to sabotage our relationship. But in retrospect, I can see this was just another lie in a long line of deceptions.

A few weeks later, he proposed. He showed up with a ring and a moving truck, ready for me to move into his house. It was all happening so fast. We had only been together for eight months, but in my vulnerability, I said yes. I was still recovering from the emotional trauma of a lengthy custody battle with my ex over my son, and I think part of me wanted stability, even if it wasn't absolute stability.

Once we were married, the truth began to unravel quickly. He owed money—more money than I had ever imagined. There were alimony payments, debts to his ex-wife, and other financial burdens that he had hidden from me. He had lost his business, and he didn't even have the credentials to run it in the first place. He wasn't the successful man I thought he was.

Then came the most significant revelation—he had another child; one he had never mentioned. He had taken a paternity test and knew about the child long before we got married, but he had kept it from me. I felt completely blindsided. How could someone hide something so significant? It was at that moment that I realized how much of our relationship had been built on lies.

My son, who had already been through so much with his own father, started to form a bond with my husband. In some ways, I think my husband was reliving his youth through my son, taking him to games and trying to be the fun, cool stepdad. But I couldn't shake the feeling that something was off. My business, my friendships, and my own sense of self were all being overshadowed by the chaos he brought into my life. I realized that I was married to someone I didn't really know. I had been so blinded by his charm, his recovery story, and my own need for stability that I had ignored all the red flags.

From the outside, everything seemed perfect. I was married, running a business, and providing for my family. But behind closed doors, my world was crumbling. The signs were always there, but I ignored them, convincing myself that things would get better, that I could fix it, that love would prevail.

When we first met, his company was small, bringing in around $300,000 a year. But I saw potential, and with hard work and determination, I helped expand it into several states and secure government contracts. We went from grossing $300,000 to landing contracts worth $33 million annually.

But with the success came more problems. Whether it was greed or carelessness, he started cheating again, and women began calling me, telling me about their affairs with him. The final blow came on my birthday, which also happens to be on Valentine's Day. It's a day you'd think your spouse would never forget, right? But he did. He missed my birthday entirely, and when he finally showed up late that night, he brought me flowers from a gas station. That's when I knew I had been holding onto a false sense of hope. And it didn't take long for the mental and verbal abuse to start. In fact, it was almost immediate.

He'd say things like, "Oh, I told you that already, don't you remember?" He'd gaslight me, insisting that conversations we never had took place or that I was forgetting important details. It was a subtle manipulation at first, designed to make me question my memory, sense of reality, and experiences. I didn't understand what was happening at the time, but slowly, I started to doubt myself.

At first, I brushed it off, thinking it was just miscommunication. But soon, I realized it was intentional—a way for him to manipulate me into doubting my own reality.

Then there was the jewelry. I had collected pieces over the years, some of which I had kept since eighth grade. They were sentimental—little treasures from different parts of my life, milestones, and memories. One day, I couldn't find them. I searched everywhere, going through drawers, closets, boxes—nothing. My immediate thought was that his daughter had stolen them. After all, she was troubled and had a difficult upbringing. Maybe she had taken them to sell or to keep for herself.

But that wasn't the truth.

When I finally left him, I found a receipt that revealed he had pawned all of my jewelry. This man, who claimed to love me and whom I had trusted, had stolen some of my most personal belongings and sold them for cash. The pain of that betrayal cut deep. It wasn't just about the jewelry itself—it was the realization that I was married to someone who could so easily deceive me.

As the lies and manipulation continued, I started to feel the weight of it all in my body. I gained 70 pounds during that time, a physical manifestation of the stress and emotional exhaustion I was experiencing. I was working relentlessly to bring back the business, ensuring that we could take care of everything in the household. I was doing everything I could to keep the marriage together because I felt like I had already failed once. Walking away from my first marriage had been hard enough, and I didn't want to go through that again.

So, I hid my pain. I cried alone in the closet because I didn't want my son to see me in such a vulnerable state. I didn't want him to think that something was wrong or that his mother couldn't hold it all together. I convinced myself that I was protecting him, shielding him from the reality of our situation. But in reality, I was crumbling on the inside.

One of the reasons I stayed in the marriage for as long as I did was because of the pressure to provide a "normal" two-parent household for my son. His father and his family had always criticized me for being a single mother and for raising a child without a father figure in the home. They made me feel like I was failing my son, like I was doing something wrong by not being part of a traditional family.

So, I thought that by marrying again, I was somehow fixing things. I was trying to prove to them—and maybe to myself—that I could provide the kind of home they deemed acceptable. But in the process, I was sacrificing my own happiness and well-being.

His daughter lived with us and came with her own set of challenges. She had been the product of his drug use and had never known her mother. She had grown up in an unstable environment, and it showed in her behavior. When I met her, she was 14, struggling with her self-esteem and weight, and not involved in typical teenage activities.

I took it upon myself to help her and give her the kind of support and care I believed she deserved. I redid her bedroom, threw her parties, and encouraged her to engage in everyday teenage life. I wanted her to feel like she belonged, like she mattered. I even took her to meet her mother and her two sisters, trying to bridge the gap that had been missing in her life.

But despite my efforts, there were deeper issues at play. She lied often and exhibited strange behavior that I later discovered was linked to Asperger's syndrome. She had been neglected emotionally for so long that she didn't know how to function in a healthy environment. There was one particularly chilling moment when she told me that her grandmother had instructed her to fight me and that sometimes she dreamed about stabbing me to death. That was when I realized the gravity of her emotional and psychological state. It was far beyond anything I had expected to deal with, and I knew I couldn't fix it alone.

One winter, just before Christmas, he called me and threatened to "come home and beat my ass." I was terrified. I had never known him to be physically violent with me, but I had my suspicions about his past. I started looking into his background, digging through court documents, and what I found shook me to my core. He had a criminal record far longer than I had imagined—19 pages of charges, including domestic abuse, drug use, and custody battles over children he hadn't even told me about.

When I found out about his second child—a child he had taken a paternity test for but never claimed—I realized how deep the lies went. I had been living in a web of deception. He wasn't just a man with a troubled past; he was still living in that chaos, dragging me and my son into it.

I did everything I could to help him and make things right. I got his record expunged, helped him rebuild his business, and handled the accounting, payroll, marketing, and hiring. I did all of the heavy lifting while he drove around, talking big, pretending to be the successful man he wasn't. And yet, he still threatened me, still disrespected me, and still cheated on me.

The night he threatened to beat me, I called my parents. They came and sat with me, waiting for him to come home. When he finally arrived, he denied everything. "I didn't say that," he insisted, gaslighting me once again. But I knew the truth. I had seen his criminal record, read through the court documents, and discovered the hidden child he had refused to acknowledge. I had spent hours in court, crying over the mess of a life he had created.

I never told him I had those documents. I carried that knowledge with me, feeling like I was harboring a secret weapon, one that I hoped I would never have to use. My father had sensed my unhappiness early on, urging me to leave, to come home. "You don't have to stay here," he would say. "You don't look happy."

But I was determined not to run from another marriage. I wanted to believe that things could be fixed and that love was enough to conquer the lies, manipulation, and darkness surrounding us.

I threw myself into trying to make our life work. I read self-help books, attended his Narcotics Anonymous (NA) meetings, and did everything I could to create a stable home for him and my son. I thought that if I could endure the worst and just hold on, at least my son would be okay. But there's only so much a person can endure before they start to break.

Our marriage lasted five and a half years, but it wasn't long before things began to deteriorate. The verbal abuse escalated into threats of physical violence.

One day, he cornered me in the bedroom after coming home. I had nowhere to go. He pinned me against the wall, his face inches from mine, yelling at me to get out of his way. "Get out of my face!" he kept saying, but I couldn't move. He had trapped me. I tried to reason with him, but before I could react, he raised his hand and mushed me in the face, fracturing my nose.

It all happened so fast. One minute, I was trying to calm him down, and the next, I was in pain, my face throbbing from the impact. My son and my two nephews were home at the time. They saw everything. Without hesitation, they jumped on him, trying to protect me. At that moment, my fear turned to rage. This man—this coward—had the audacity to not only hurt me but to call the police and file a report against the children for attacking him.

Thankfully, I knew the local police officers, and when they told me what he had done, I was able to intervene. I warned him that if he didn't fix the situation, I would call their fathers, and he knew exactly what that meant. He dropped the charges, but the damage had already been done. The physical abuse, the betrayal, the lies—it was all starting to come to the surface.

The abuse wasn't just physical. It was emotional, psychological, and, at times, humiliating. He had this need to be the center of attention, always to be the loudest and most noticeable person in the room. I remember one particular incident when he invited me to a concert. It was an event we used to attend every year, and he insisted that we sit in the front row. I didn't want to go. Our relationship was in shambles, and the last thing I wanted was to pretend that everything was fine in front of a crowd of strangers. But he pushed, and I reluctantly agreed.

We sat next to another couple, and I noticed something strange from the moment we arrived. The woman sitting next to me refused to acknowledge me. She didn't speak to me, didn't look at me, nothing. It was awkward, to say the least. By the end of the night, I had a sinking feeling in my stomach.

I turned to him and said, "That's the woman you've been cheating with, isn't it? Does her husband know?"

His face went pale. "Stop it," he hissed, trying to shut me down. But I wasn't backing off. I was tired of the lies. I was tired of being humiliated. I leaned over to the woman and asked her point-blank if her husband knew about their affair. She didn't flinch. "I don't have to sneak around," she said, her voice cold and unapologetic. "He knows what I do."

I was stunned. This woman, sitting next to her husband, had no shame, no remorse. I left the concert in tears, feeling more broken than I ever had before.

After that, things only got worse. I became nocturnal, unable to sleep at night for fear that he would wake up the house or start another argument. He would come home at odd hours, always demanding my attention, constantly stirring up chaos. I started sleeping on the floor at the foot of our bed, hoping that he wouldn't make a scene if I were at least in the room. But that didn't work either. The fear of what he might do next consumed me, and I began staying up all night, working to keep my mind occupied.

There was one night, in particular, when he had pushed me to my limit. I had had surgery earlier that week and was still recovering, but he didn't care. He demanded that I get up and handle payroll, ignoring the fact that I was in pain and needed rest. He was completely indifferent to my needs. All that mattered to him was that the work got done. I had already completed payroll, but his lack of concern for my well-being was just another reminder of how little he valued me.

The breaking point came when I found out he was cheating on me again, this time with a woman he had met through one of our business contracts. It wasn't the first time, and I knew it wouldn't be the last. But this time, I couldn't stay silent. I confronted him, and of course, he denied everything, twisting the truth as he always did. But I had reached my limit.

I made him get a job, thinking that things might get better if he was at least working. But they didn't. He continued to lie, cheat, and manipulate. His daughter even told me that his mother was allowing him to spend the night with the other woman at her house. It was a betrayal on every level. Not only was he unfaithful, but his own family was complicit in his deceit.

There comes a moment in every person's life when they realize that enough is enough. For me, that moment came when I knew I could no longer endure the life I was living. My son had graduated from high school, and the timing couldn't have been better. He was preparing to leave for college, and the house was still full of the noise and laughter of his friends coming by to say their goodbyes. But all of that abruptly stopped when my husband declared that no one could come over anymore.

"No one is allowed in the house. I don't want to see anyone here. And you better not let anybody come by," he told me, his tone dripping with menace. At that moment, the weight of his attempt to isolate me hit me like a ton of bricks. I felt trapped, like a prisoner in my own home. His goal was clear—he wanted me alone, afraid, and utterly dependent on him.

I filed for a restraining order shortly after that. The escalating threats had pushed me into survival mode, and I needed a way out. We had a conversation, and I made it clear that I was leaving, that I was done. But even then, his manipulation didn't stop. "You're not going anywhere," he told me. "You don't have anyone. You have nowhere to go."

Despite his attempts to intimidate me, I stood firm. But I hesitated when he begged me to drop the restraining order because it would ruin his business credentials. I thought to myself, "Maybe I don't need to be this cruel." So, I foolishly agreed to drop it. That same day, he turned around and filed one against me.

That was the final straw. I knew I had to leave for good this time. My sister and her friends came to help me gather a few things from the house, and while we were there, he sat on the couch as if nothing had happened, calling the next woman in line. "I finally got her out. Do you still need a place to stay?" His audacity left me speechless, but I knew I had made the right decision.

Let's rewind a bit because before I left, there were other signs—big ones—that he was unraveling. We had multiple cars, including his and hers Mercedes-Benz. I had always paid the car payments, but after learning about his infidelities, I decided I wouldn't pay for his lifestyle anymore. "I'm not going to keep paying for you to drive women around in a car I pay for," I told him.

Not long after, he wrecked the car on purpose. I know it was intentional because when I visited him in the hospital, his words didn't match the scene he described. "I won't do it again," he said. My son and I exchanged a look—this wasn't someone who had just been in an accident; this was someone who had staged one. I sent my son to check the supposed crash site, and there was nothing—no debris, no skid marks, no sign of an accident. When I saw the car at the junkyard, it was clear he had run it into a pole.

This behavior became the norm. He'd get caught cheating, threaten to harm me, and then go back to his manipulative games.

Another time, he called me and said, "I'm going to beat you when I get home." But he stayed quiet when he arrived and saw that my children were there. His threats became a routine part of my life, but I refused to live in fear anymore.

The night I left was chaotic. I didn't take much—just a few of my son's things and whatever I could grab at the moment. I thought I would be able to return the next day to collect the rest of my belongings. But when I went back, he had already changed the locks. He had called the police, and that's when I found out he had filed a restraining order against me. I was left with nothing—no furniture, no clothes, just the few items I had taken with me when I walked out the door.

I stayed with my parents for a while, trying to figure out what to do next. One night, he called me, saying we needed to talk about getting back together. Naively, I agreed to meet him, hoping to resolve things amicably.

But it was a setup. The real reason he wanted me there was to take back the key to one of the Mercedeses. When I refused to hand it over—because the car was in my name—he lost it.

He pinned me to the floor, his hands wrapped around my wrists as he banged my head against the ground, trying to pry the keys from my grip. In the process, he fractured both of my hands. He got the keys, but the damage was done—physically and emotionally. The police were called, but since I had left the house first, I was the one with limited rights to return. I couldn't believe the situation I was in. He had turned everything upside down.

The extent of his deceit went beyond our personal lives. While we were going through the divorce proceedings, I found out that he had been following my son, taking pictures of him at various places, and building a case against him. He wanted my son arrested for the fight that had occurred when my son was 16, even though my son had only been defending me. This man, who had once claimed to love my child as his own, was now trying to destroy his life out of spite.

It didn't stop there. He began dating a woman I had known since sixth grade, someone I had considered a friend. Together, they committed identity theft against me. They opened bank accounts in my name, wrote fraudulent checks, and dragged me through financial hell. I was forced to get a new driver's license number and was even offered a new Social Security number due to the severity of the identity theft.

The police reports he filed were outrageous. He claimed that I was stalking him, standing outside his window in freezing weather, trying to make him talk to me. The truth was, I wanted nothing to do with him. I was terrified of him, ashamed of the life I had allowed myself to fall into. But he continued to lie, trying to paint himself as the victim.

On top of everything else, he drained my bank account. He withdrew over $10,000, leaving me with nothing. When I confronted him, he had the nerve to tell me it was my responsibility to go to the bank and take his name off our joint account. I was too afraid not to comply, but the bank staff knew what was happening. They refused to let me make any changes and escorted me out through the back to avoid him.

He did everything in his power to ruin me—emotionally, financially, and even socially. While I was trying to rebuild my life, he continued to make false police reports, accusing me of things I hadn't done. But thanks to a police officer friend, I learned that his lies didn't hold up. Cell tower records showed he wasn't even in the locations where he claimed I was stalking him. The evidence was clear—this man was a master manipulator, a sociopath who thrived on destroying the lives of those around him.

As we moved through the divorce proceedings, the ugliness of his character became more and more apparent. He wasn't just fighting me—he was fighting my son.

He wanted my son arrested, charged, and punished for standing up to him. But my son had done nothing wrong. He had only ever been a good kid, someone who had never been in trouble a day in his life. And yet, here we were, with this man trying to destroy him, just as he had wanted to destroy me.

It took years to untangle myself from the web of lies and manipulation he had spun around me. But slowly, I began to rebuild. I fought back, not just for myself, but for my son and everyone else he had tried to hurt. The process wasn't easy, and the scars will always remain, but I came out stronger, wiser, and more determined than ever, never to let anyone control me again.

There's a strange mix of relief and sadness that comes with leaving an abusive relationship. Relief is because you've finally escaped the torment, and sadness is because of the time and energy you've lost trying to make it work. I lost years of my life to that man, years that I'll never get back. But I gained something far more valuable—freedom.

The freedom to live on my own terms, to rebuild from the ground up, and finally find peace. It wasn't an easy road, but it was a necessary one. And as I look back on everything I went through, I realize just how strong I am. Strong enough to survive, strong enough to fight back, and strong enough to reclaim my life.

When you first fall in love with someone, you believe in the good. You see their best version and hold onto that, hoping that any flaws or red flags are just temporary setbacks—things that love, patience, and time can fix. But love alone can't fix everything. In fact, sometimes love closes your eyes to the reality you're living in.

My marriage was a far cry from what I had imagined it to be. There was no honeymoon phase and no smooth adjustment period. From the start, there were red flags. But I stayed. I stayed for my son. I stayed because I believed in the good in people, and I stayed because I thought I could fix it.

It started small—subtle lies, strange behaviors. He was always a little off, but I told myself it was just the remnants of his past. He had been clean for years when we met, so I believed he had left that part of his life behind. But addiction doesn't just vanish. The personality traits, the habits, and the erratic behavior often linger long after the substances are gone.

Then came the lies about his background. He was ashamed of where he came from, and he lied about it often. He pretended to be someone he wasn't, hiding parts of his past that he thought I wouldn't accept. But it wasn't his past that was the problem; it was his dishonesty. Over time, the small lies became bigger, and I started to see the cracks in the facade he had built.

His behavior became more erratic as time went on. He was constantly doing things that didn't make sense, like the time he burned his hand trying to mow the lawn. I had asked him to handle the yard work since I would no longer pay for a gardener. Instead of just doing the job, he somehow managed to burn his hand on the lawnmower engine severely. To this day, I don't know how it happened. I remember asking him, "Did you just hold your hand there?" The whole situation was bizarre.

But that was just one example of many. He was careless, destructive, and constantly breaking things around the house. He once destroyed a brand-new dining room table I had just bought.

And then there was the hair dye. For months, I kept finding black stains all over the bathroom—on the counters, the floor, the towels. I had no idea where it came from until I discovered that he had secretly dyed his hair. He hid the dye in a suitcase as if this were something to be ashamed of. It was yet another example of how he was constantly hiding things from me, even the most trivial details.

The financial aspect of our relationship was another source of constant stress. He relied on me to handle everything—payroll, bills, the business. I ran the entire show while he enjoyed the lifestyle that I had built. But when I finally started pulling back, refusing to pay for his luxuries, he retaliated. He would drain my bank accounts, leaving me with nothing.

I went to my parents' house, feeling like a failure but also knowing that I had made the right decision. I had finally escaped.

Leaving him was the hardest thing I've ever done, but it was also the most liberating. My health had suffered tremendously during the marriage—my hair was falling out, I had gained weight, and my immune system had begun to attack itself, leading to a diagnosis of lupus. My doctor told me it was stress-related, and I have no doubt that my marriage was the cause.

The moment I left, I began to heal. My mother noticed it immediately—within days, I had lost weight, my hair started to grow back, and the light returned to my eyes. It was as if a dark cloud had been lifted, and for the first time in years, I could breathe again.

If there's one piece of advice I can give to anyone reading this, it's to speak up sooner. Don't wait for things to get worse. Don't wait for the next big disaster. If you see the signs, listen to them. Trust your instincts and know that it's okay to walk away. Your well-being—your life—is worth so much more than staying in a toxic relationship.

Chapter 8
Learning to Move On

For almost ten years, I was stuck. Stuck in the fear, humiliation, and scarcity brought on by my past relationships, particularly my second marriage, which left the deepest scars. It took a significant toll on me, so much so that I lost a part of myself, the part that knew what it meant to feel worthy. I struggled to communicate with others, to connect, and even to find the self-esteem I once had.

I was paralyzed by the past, unable to let go of the weight it carried. There were days, even weeks, when I wouldn't leave the house at all. The things that once brought me joy and a sense of purpose—shopping, socializing, even simple activities like taking a walk—became distant memories. I would drive miles out of my way to shop at grocery stores far from home to avoid running into anyone I might know. The fear wasn't just of being judged or humiliated by those who knew my story. It was a fear of the unknown—of who knew what, of who might have been part of my story without my even realizing it. The paranoia consumed me.

I felt like I was living in a self-imposed exile, trapped by the fear of bad reputations, harmful words, or painful reminders of what had happened. I missed out on life, moments of joy, and watching my child grow and evolve. I, myself, was unable to grow. I couldn't move forward because I was stuck in a cycle of reliving the trauma over and over again.

The past was my prison, and the door was locked from the inside.

To move on, I realized something had to change. There's a saying: To be something different, you have to do something different. So, I started small. I had to learn to dig myself out of the hole I had been buried in, step by step. I had to accept that sometimes, the lessons we know aren't even meant for us—they're lessons from someone else's journey that we just happen to be a part of. I was caught in someone else's storm, but that didn't mean I had to stay there.

Family, relationships, even friends—they can all be part of a generational cycle of dysfunction. I had to grow past that. I had to be forward-thinking, to look ahead and not cling to the past. There's a reason why we're always told not to look back unless it's to learn. The past doesn't hold the keys to the future, and I had to accept that not everything behind me needed to come with me.

Being stuck. I can't even begin to describe the weight of that word. It's not just a mental or emotional block—it's a full-body experience. It keeps you in place and paralyzes you from living the life you deserve. That's exactly where I found myself.

I knew I needed to shift my focus to stop replaying the same traumatic memories over and over again. My brain kept dragging me back, but I had to fight against it. Complacency was my enemy. If I allowed myself to remain still, I would never get out.

So, what did I do? I forced myself to act. Whether it was taking a simple walk outside or doing something I used to love, I found little ways to bring myself back to the present. Meditation affirmations—these were tools I used to retrain my mind. They helped me change my thoughts, which eventually helped me change my outlook.

I had to remember that I was the priority. By focusing on myself and making *me* my first priority, I no longer had time or energy to dwell on the past. Slowly but surely, I started finding joy again. It wasn't easy, and it wasn't quick, but every small step counted.

I've always believed that complacency is one of the most dangerous places a person can find themselves in. It doesn't just creep up on you—it envelops you slowly, like a fog, making you lose sight of what's ahead. I found myself there after my second marriage, lost in the fear, humiliation, and self-doubt that followed. I was stuck, and for nearly ten years, I struggled to rediscover the person I used to be.

The complacency wasn't just mental; it seeped into every part of my life. Getting out of bed, going outside, and interacting with others—all became monumental tasks. I had dreams once, a desire to achieve something more, but that fire dimmed. I became someone who gave 200% just to get the bare minimum. When I managed to get that job without a degree, I threw myself into it, pushing beyond my limits but always feeling like it wasn't enough. The past, the trauma, and the weight of it all were still holding me back.

For years, I was driven by survival mode, trying to prove my worth through relentless hard work, but that didn't erase the fact that I was stuck. The complacency came from a place of fear, of not wanting to confront the past or even the present. I stayed in my comfort zone, thinking it would protect me. But all it did was prevent me from living, from growing. I had to face the uncomfortable truth: I wasn't truly living, just existing.

That saying stuck with me: To be something different, you have to do something different. That's what I had to remind myself of every day when I realized I was stagnating. I had to rediscover that inner drive to achieve, to push past the limits I had unknowingly set for myself. It wasn't easy. There were days when I couldn't even bring myself to leave the house. I would avoid places where I might see familiar faces, terrified of judgment, of humiliation, of reliving the stories I wanted so desperately to leave behind.

But there comes a point when you realize that standing still doesn't protect you. It just keeps you chained to the very things you're trying to escape. I had to start small—baby steps. I forced myself to act, even when I didn't want to. Even if it felt foreign at first. I began journaling, reflecting on the times when I had felt the happiest, and looking for ways to recapture that sense of purpose.

Complacency tricks you into thinking that change is impossible. But the truth is, the only way out is through action. I had to acknowledge my past, not just the trauma, but the way I handled it. For the longest time, I blamed myself for staying in toxic relationships and for allowing things to happen. That blame weighed me down, making it harder to forgive and move forward. But eventually, I had to make peace with it. I had to learn self-compassion to understand that I wasn't just a victim of others—I was also holding myself captive by refusing to let go.

The process wasn't just about me, though. I learned to seek support when I needed it, realizing that sometimes, you can't carry the burden alone. Whether it was through therapy or talking to someone who truly understood my experiences, I found that sharing the load made it lighter. But finding the right kind of help wasn't easy. It took time to build trust again, especially after years of feeling like no one truly understood me. It wasn't always family or close friends who could help, but finding someone whose values aligned with mine made a world of difference.

But it wasn't just the external weight of the world pressing down on me. I was struggling to forgive myself, and that made it even harder to believe that God could forgive me, either. I spent many sleepless nights praying, crying out for some kind of sign, some kind of relief. And through those nights of desperation, something shifted. I felt God's presence in a way I hadn't felt in a long time. He showed me that His love was stanch and that I wasn't defined by the pain or the mistakes of my past.

I realized that I wasn't a reflection of what had happened to me. God had never intended for me to stay stuck in those memories, replaying them like a broken record. He began showing me that my future—this present moment—was far more valuable than anything I had endured. The past was over. Whether it was a day, a month, or a year ago, it was done. And as long as I held onto it, I was robbing myself of the life that God was offering me right now.

God has always taken care of me, even in my darkest moments. There were times I thought I couldn't possibly endure another heartbreak, another disappointment, but each time, He pulled me through. My faith became my anchor, and I found strength in knowing that God was my refuge. He was my protector, the one I could turn to at any hour of the day or night. With that certainty, I began to look toward the future, slowly regaining hope and the courage to keep moving forward.

Sometimes, when we go through trauma, we lose sight of that. We forget that God is still there, still holding us up, waiting for us to come back to Him. But when you do, when you remember that He is your friend, your guide, everything starts to shift. The future no longer looks bleak. It becomes something bright, something you can actually reach for again.

I started to see that the worst moments of my life weren't meant to define me. They were part of my story, yes, but they weren't the end. They weren't my identity. God didn't put me here to suffer or to be trapped in my past. He gave me life so that I could grow, learn, and move forward.

In the grand scheme of things, we're all just a tiny part of this vast universe. Like astronauts often say when they look back at Earth from space, our problems, our pain—they're so small. From up there, everything that seems overwhelming here feels like just a blip. That doesn't mean it's meaningless, though. It's just a reminder that we are part of something much bigger, and while our pain is real, it isn't the end of the world.

God, in all His infinite wisdom, knows every single one of us—right down to the number of hairs on our heads. He knows our struggles and our fears, and He hasn't abandoned us. He doesn't want us to stay stuck, reliving the same trauma over and over again. There's more for us than that. He didn't create us just to suffer.

We all face a choice when we're caught in the grip of our past. You can either confront your pain, deal with the consequences, and move on, or you can stay stuck. You can watch the world pass by, stuck in the same place, while everything else moves forward without you. I've been there, caught in that paralysis. And I chose to act. I chose to forgive myself, to seek help, and to trust in God's plan for me.

I've been there. I've been complacent, stuck in my past. But life doesn't allow you to stay there forever—not without consequence. When you refuse to let go and move on, you end up living in that stagnant space where growth, experience, and opportunity pass you by. I've come to realize that complacency is a kind of slow death. It isn't the kind of death where your heart stops beating, but a slow fade where your dreams, your ambitions, and your ability to live fully wither away.

The odds were always stacked against me. I didn't have a degree when I got my first significant job, but that didn't stop me. I worked twice as hard, gave 200% of myself, and refused to accept mediocrity. I landed a six-figure position as a Director of HR despite the odds. I was young, I was Black, I was a woman—and I didn't have the degree they were looking for. But what I had was a fire inside me, a determination to succeed. I walked into that position like I was heaven-sent, and I made them believe in me.

Life will always present opportunities—sometimes subtle, sometimes glaring. The problem is that many people are so consumed by their past failures or traumas that they can't see the opportunities when they come. They're trapped in this negative mindset, convinced that nothing good will ever happen to them. I've seen it time and time again: people stuck in their misery because it's comfortable, because it's all they've known. And, as they say, misery loves company.

But there's always a way out if you're willing to take it. Sometimes, your mindset is the only thing standing between you and your future. Opportunities may knock, but if you're stuck in your past, you won't be able to open the door.

I've learned to embrace new experiences and celebrate my progress, no matter how small. Self-compassion became a vital part of my journey. It's hard to move forward when you're constantly punishing yourself for the mistakes you've made. But forgiveness—both of yourself and others—is crucial. You have to realize that the past is over. It's done.

You can't change it, but you can choose not to be trapped by it.

There's a quote that has stayed with me: "If you can't fly, then run. If you can't run, then walk. If you can't walk, then crawl. But whatever you do, you have to keep moving forward." Those words by Martin Luther King Jr. remind me that forward motion, no matter how small, is what keeps us alive and growing.

The truth is, unless you let go—unless you forgive yourself, forgive the situation, and realize that it's over—you can't move forward. Staying stuck is a choice, but so is moving on. And that's what I had to choose.

I also found comfort in my faith. God doesn't burden us with more than we can bear, and that thought stayed with me through the hardest moments. There were times when I felt like I was at rock bottom, but even then, I knew deep down that I wasn't abandoned. I had to trust that God had a plan for me, that He hadn't left me to suffer without purpose. It's easy to lose sight of that when life is throwing one storm after another at you, but faith, for me, became a lifeline.

Moving on, for me, didn't just mean leaving the past behind—it meant understanding that the pain and mistakes were part of my story, but they weren't the whole story. God didn't put me here to be stuck. He gave me the strength to move forward, even when it felt impossible.

In the end, you have two choices: you either stay stuck in the past, paralyzed by your mistakes, or you act. You pick yourself up, dust yourself off, and take that first step, however small, toward something better. It's not easy, and it takes time. But trust me, once you start moving forward, the path ahead becomes clearer, and you'll find that life still has so much more to offer.

You just have to be willing to step into it.

Chapter 9
Finding My Voice (Again)

Leaving him felt like escaping a burning building—scarred, breathless, but alive. I emerged from that smoke-filled wreckage not as a victim, but as a survivor still covered in ash but walking tall. My spirit was cracked but unbroken. Homeless, heart-worn, and starting over, I had something this time I didn't have before: clarity. I had seen behind the curtain of manipulation and lies, and I was done being quiet.

No more whispering my truths. No more apologizing for surviving. I had let too many people narrate my story, twist my worth into something disposable. But I had receipts. I had memory. And I had the will to speak up. I started small—telling friends the truth behind the bruises. Then lawyers. Police. Judges. Every time I said it out loud, the fear loosened its grip a little more.

But finding my voice wasn't just about confronting him. It was about remembering me. I rediscovered my laugh, the way music moved me, the way I loved being barefoot in the kitchen, making my grandma's recipes. I took back the colors I wore, the music I danced to, the freedom to flirt again, to love again—especially to love me.

There were days I wanted to hide again. Days when the mirror only showed a woman full of doubt. But she, too, was brave. She still got up, still showed up. That woman—me—

was no longer defined by what had been done to her. She was defined by how she rose.

"Your voice is your power—when you find it, never let it go."

Complacency can creep into your life like an invisible fog, slow and suffocating. It disguises itself as a safe haven, a comfortable space where the weight of change and challenge doesn’t touch you. But beneath that false sense of security lies stagnation—a slow death of ambition, dreams, and self-worth.

For ten years, I lived in the shadow of complacency. It wasn’t intentional. I didn’t wake up one day and decide to put my life on pause. It happened gradually, starting with the mental, emotional, and even physical tolls of an abusive relationship. I’d been beaten down—psychologically and then physically—to the point where the stress consumed me. It was easier to stay in the comfort zone of “just getting by” than to face the daunting task of starting over. But what I thought was comfort was actually a prison.

Complacency feels deceptively safe. You tell yourself that you don’t need to dream bigger, that your current circumstances are “enough.” But over time, you lose sight of your true potential. You stop envisioning a future that excites you. The dreams you once had—retiring at 47, living a life of financial security and freedom—become distant memories. Instead, you find yourself stuck, replaying the same patterns, reliving past mistakes, and feeling as though you’re trapped in a cycle you can’t escape.

I liken complacency to a stagnant pond. On the surface, it might appear serene, with lily pads and flowers floating peacefully. But beneath that stillness lies murky, lifeless water. The same is true for life when you let complacency take over. You might look fine on the outside, but inside, there's no growth, no movement, no vibrancy. And the longer you stay in that stagnant state, the harder it becomes to break free.

The stress of complacency doesn't just weigh on your mind; it wreaks havoc on your body. For me, the years of unresolved stress and emotional turmoil led to significant health issues. My immune system began to attack itself, and I was diagnosed with lupus—a condition my doctor directly attributed to stress. I gained weight, lost hair, and felt my energy drain away. It was as though my body was physically manifesting the toll of staying stuck for so long. And yet, even as my health deteriorated, I clung to complacency because it felt easier than confronting the pain. I avoided journaling, a practice that had always brought me clarity and healing, because I didn't want to face the memories. I told myself that it was safer to stay in my bubble to avoid risking further disappointment or failure. But all I was doing was depriving myself of growth and happiness.

Breaking free from complacency isn't easy. It requires uncomfortable action—a willingness to face the fear and uncertainty you've been avoiding. For me, the first steps were small but significant. I began journaling again, forcing myself to confront the emotions and memories I had tried to bury. I sought out new experiences—joining groups of supportive women, exploring meditation and affirmations, and rediscovering activities that brought me joy.

One of the biggest shifts came when I realized that complacency wasn't protecting me but holding me back. I had convinced myself that staying in my comfort zone was the safest option, but in reality, it was a barrier to everything I wanted. I had to let go of the fear of failure and the desire for absolute security to move forward. I had to embrace the discomfort of growth.

There's a saying that has stuck with me: "To be something different, you have to do something different." This became my mantra as I worked to break free from the habits and mindsets that had kept me stuck. I had to challenge myself to think and act differently, even when it felt unnatural. For example, I began seeking opportunities that I might have overlooked before. I pushed myself to connect with people outside of my usual circles to explore perspectives and practices that were unfamiliar to me.

This included stepping outside the boundaries of what I'd been taught in church or at home and embracing new ideas that resonated with my evolving sense of self. At the same time, I focused on rebuilding my confidence and rediscovering my ambition. For years, I'd felt dismissed and overlooked in my personal relationships and career. But I refused to let those experiences define me.

I reminded myself of the times when I had defied expectations—landing a Director of HR position without a degree, turning mid-level companies into lucrative enterprises, and working tirelessly to achieve success despite the odds.

Being in a toxic relationship had stripped me of my self-worth. I'd internalized the negative messages I'd received, convincing myself that I wasn't good enough or strong enough to succeed on my own. Society's expectations and stereotypes only added to that burden, making it even harder to believe in myself. But as I worked to break free from complacency, I began to reclaim my identity. I rediscovered the ambitious, determined woman I had always been.

I reminded myself that I could overcome obstacles and achieve my goals. And I committed to showing others that it was possible to rise above adversity and create a life you're proud of.

Breaking free from complacency isn't a one-time decision; it's an ongoing process. It requires daily effort to push past the fear and self-doubt that can creep back in. But every step forward—no matter how small—brings you closer to the life you deserve. For me, the journey involved redefining success and embracing a new mindset. I learned to celebrate progress, no matter how incremental, and to focus on what I could control. Not just that, I also leaned on my faith, trusting that God had a plan for me. I had a strong belief that He would guide me through the challenges I faced.

The fight to break free from complacency also meant reevaluating the relationships in my life. I had to distance myself from people who fed into my sense of stagnation or who couldn't understand my need for change. This wasn't easy; some of these people had been in my life for years. But I realized that if I wanted to grow, I needed to surround myself with individuals who supported that growth. I found solace in the company of women who shared similar experiences, knew what it was like to feel stuck, and had also fought their way out. These women became a lifeline, offering encouragement and reminding me that I wasn't alone in my struggles.

I also had to confront the internal narratives that had kept me stuck for so long.

I had convinced myself that I couldn't achieve more, that my past mistakes defined me, and that it was safer to stay in my comfort zone than risk failure. These beliefs were like chains, holding me back from pursuing the life I wanted. It took time and effort to dismantle these narratives, replacing them with affirmations and a renewed belief in my own potential.

There were moments when I doubted myself when the fear of stepping outside my comfort zone felt overwhelming. But each time, I reminded myself of the progress I had already made.

I looked back on the small victories—journaling again, joining new groups, taking on challenges at work—and used them as motivation to keep going. I learned to celebrate these wins, no matter how minor they seemed, because they were proof that I was moving forward.

Faith played a crucial role in my journey. There were times when I felt like giving up when the weight of my past and the uncertainty of the future felt too heavy to bear.

But in those moments, I turned to God, seeking guidance and strength.

I reminded myself that I wasn't alone, that there was a plan for my life, even if I couldn't see it yet. This faith gave me the courage to take risks, step into the unknown, and trust that I could overcome whatever challenges lay ahead.

As I continued to break free from complacency, I began to see the world in a new light. Opportunities that had once seemed out of reach now felt attainable. I started dreaming again, imagining a future filled with possibilities rather than limitations.

I set new goals for myself, both personally and professionally, and began taking steps to achieve them. This wasn't an overnight transformation but a gradual process filled with setbacks and challenges. But with each step forward, I felt more empowered and more confident in my ability to create the life I wanted.

Complacency might feel safe in the moment, but it's a trap that keeps you from living fully. By taking action and believing in yourself, you can break free and create a life filled with purpose and possibility. It's not easy, but it's worth it. And if I can do it, so can you.

Chapter 10
The Power of Forgiveness (and a Little Bit of Lipstick)

Forgiveness is like drinking water in a desert after surviving on resentment for years. I thought holding on to anger gave me power—it felt like armor. But in truth, it was a prison. Every ounce of hatred I carried for him was a brick I stacked around myself.

Forgiving him didn't mean forgetting. It didn't mean excusing. It meant letting go. It meant choosing me over the pain. It meant releasing myself from replaying the scenes that broke me.

But forgiving myself? Whew. That was the real journey. I had to let go of the guilt—the guilt of staying too long, of trusting too easily, of loving someone broken while I was still trying to heal myself. I had to unlearn the shame he wrapped around me like a second skin. And I did. Slowly. Painfully. Beautifully.

I found joy in the smallest things again. Lipstick became my armor—fiery red lips on a day when I needed to feel alive. Music blasting as I danced in my kitchen. Long phone calls with girlfriends who saw me, heard me, and loved me.

Forgiveness cracked the window open, and joy blew in like a summer breeze.

"Forgiveness is the fragrance the violet sheds on the heel that has crushed it."

— Mark Twain

Trauma is a profound, life-altering experience that defies simple explanation. It is not just the moment of crisis or the event itself but the lasting imprint it leaves on the mind, body, and soul. To some, trauma manifests as a sudden, seismic shift that shakes the foundation of their world. For others, it is a slow, creeping erosion of safety and trust, accumulating over time until it becomes impossible to ignore. Regardless of how it is experienced, trauma reshapes your understanding of life, your perception of yourself, and the way you interact with the world.

What makes trauma so challenging to define is its deeply personal nature. Two people could face the same event and respond in entirely different ways. For one, it might become a pivotal moment of pain and transformation; for another, it may pass as a difficult but manageable experience. This variability doesn't diminish the impact of trauma—it highlights its complexity.

Clinically, trauma is described as an emotional response to a deeply distressing or disturbing event, one that overwhelms an individual's ability to cope.

It can be the result of a singular event, such as an accident or an assault, or the culmination of repeated experiences, such as ongoing abuse or neglect. Yet, beyond the clinical definitions, trauma is profoundly personal. It is the gap between what we expect from life and what we are forced to endure. It is the loss of control, the shattering of assumptions, and the deep questioning of what it means to feel safe and whole.

For me, trauma arrived unexpectedly, like an unwelcome guest who barged into my life and refused to leave. Growing up, I had a limited understanding of what trauma could look like.

Though not without its challenges, my life had been largely free from the kinds of upheavals that leave lasting scars. But when trauma finally found me, it did so with a force I was utterly unprepared for. It disrupted everything I thought I knew about myself and the world around me. It was a lesson in vulnerability, one I never sought but could not avoid.

What I've come to understand is that trauma does not come with a rulebook. It does not ask for permission, nor does it wait for you to be ready.

It simply happens, leaving you to grapple with its aftermath. It can leave you feeling lost, unsure of who you are or how to navigate the world. But in this chaos, there is also the potential for growth, a deeper understanding of yourself, and discovering the strength you never knew you had.

In the end, the true essence of trauma lies not just in the pain it brings but in the transformation it demands. It forces you to confront the unthinkable, to rebuild from the ashes, and to find a new sense of meaning and purpose. And while the journey is never easy, it reveals the resilience of the human spirit and the capacity to heal and thrive despite the weight of the past.

Trauma, especially when endured by women, reshapes not only the way they perceive the world but also how they see themselves. It leaves a mark far deeper than the visible scars—it rewires thoughts, emotions, and even the body. For many women, trauma is not a singular event but a layered experience compounded by societal expectations, cultural norms, and the unspoken weight of silence.

When trauma strikes, it chips away at the foundational beliefs women hold about safety, trust, and control. It rewrites the narrative of who they are, often instilling feelings of doubt and insecurity where there was once confidence and stability.

The changes trauma brings can be so pervasive that even the simplest aspects of daily life can feel foreign. Suddenly, the world seems less predictable, and interactions that were once effortless now carry the burden of anxiety and fear.

Physically, trauma can manifest in a myriad of ways. Women may experience chronic fatigue, tension headaches, digestive issues, or unexplained pain that serves as a constant reminder of the battles they've faced. In some cases, the body may turn against itself, leading to autoimmune diseases, weight fluctuations, or even hair loss, as if the trauma is trying to escape through physical symptoms.

Emotionally, the changes are equally profound. Trauma often robs women of their sense of emotional safety, making vulnerability feel like a risk they can no longer afford to take. Trust becomes fragile, and relationships—whether with friends, family, or partners—may bear the brunt of this newfound caution. Anxiety can weave itself into the fabric of their lives, accompanied by persistent feelings of unease and a hyperawareness of potential threats.

For some women, trauma silences them, leaving them trapped within their own minds, unable to articulate the depth of their pain. For others, it triggers a fight for survival, forcing them to confront parts of themselves they never knew existed. In either case, the woman they once were begins to fade, replaced by someone who has been irrevocably changed.

But perhaps the most heart-wrenching transformation lies in the loss of innocence—the realization that the world, as they once knew it, is no longer safe or fair. Trauma takes the luxury of naivety from women, replacing it with an acute awareness of life's unpredictability. It reshapes their boundaries, their coping mechanisms, and even their hopes for the future.

Despite this, women continue to endure, adapt, and evolve. The changes trauma imposes are not always easy to reconcile, but they are a testament to the resilience and strength that lie within. While the scars of trauma may never fully fade, they often become reminders of the battles fought and the courage it takes to keep moving forward.

Trauma for many women often carries the added weight of enduring both mental and physical abuse, experiences that intertwine to create an overwhelming cycle of pain and fear. Abuse rarely begins with obvious violence; instead, it creeps into a woman's life, starting with subtle manipulation, dismissive words, or actions that seem inconsequential at first. Over time, however, these moments escalate, becoming patterns of control and harm that reshape her world.

Mental abuse, though less visible than physical violence, often strikes deeper wounds. It begins with words that linger, embedding themselves into the fabric of a woman's thoughts. Small, biting remarks can accumulate, turning into a steady stream of criticism and blame, leaving her to question her worth and reality.

This kind of abuse thrives on isolation, gradually separating her from her support systems and convincing her that she has nowhere else to turn. Over time, this mental erosion creates a landscape of doubt, where even her instincts and feelings are unreliable.

The toll of such abuse is profound. Women find themselves walking on eggshells, constantly trying to anticipate the next verbal assault. This heightened state of vigilance saps emotional and mental energy, leaving little room for anything beyond survival.

Dreams, ambitions, and even simple joys shrink in the shadow of the abuse, replaced by a heavy sense of inadequacy and fear. The repeated cycles of manipulation and gaslighting lead many to blame themselves, believing they are the cause of the harm inflicted upon them.

Physical abuse, while more overt, carries its own devastating impact. The immediate injuries—bruises, broken bones, or other visible scars—are only part of the story. The pain goes deeper, often becoming a constant reminder of the violence endured.

Yet, even when the physical wounds heal, the psychological scars linger, manifesting as chronic pain, sleep disturbances, or an unshakable feeling of vulnerability. For many, the body becomes a site of betrayal, a reminder of their powerlessness in moments of violence.

Together, mental and physical abuse create a vicious cycle, one that traps women in a web of fear and helplessness. The two forms of harm often reinforce each other, with physical violence used to silence resistance and mental abuse ensuring submission. Many women endure these conditions for years, unable to leave due to fear, financial dependence, or the deep psychological hold abusers often maintain over their victims.

What is perhaps most insidious about abuse is the way it alters a woman's sense of self. Over time, she may begin to see herself through the eyes of her abuser, believing the cruel words and internalizing the violence. The abuse distorts her identity, leaving her disconnected from the person she once was. Relationships, once sources of comfort and trust, become fraught with doubt and anxiety. Even after escaping the abusive environment, the emotional residue remains, making it difficult to rebuild trust, form new connections, or feel safe in the world.

These experiences underscore the profound and lasting impact of trauma, showing how deeply it can reshape the lives of those who endure it.

Yet, within this darkness, there is also resilience—a quiet strength that many women carry as they navigate the complexities of survival and recovery. The process of healing may be long and arduous, but it is also a testament to their enduring spirit and the capacity to rise above even the most devastating circumstances.

Overcoming trauma is neither a straight path nor a journey with a clear endpoint, but it is possible. For women who have faced the depths of pain caused by mental and physical abuse, the process of healing is as individual as the trauma itself. It begins with a single step—acknowledging the hurt and recognizing that they deserve more than the suffering they have endured.

Healing often starts with the act of seeking help, whether through therapy, support groups, or even confiding in a trusted friend or family member. Therapy can provide a safe space to process the complex emotions trauma leaves behind, offering tools to untangle the narratives imposed by abuse and replace them with ones rooted in self-worth and empowerment. For some, support groups create a community where shared experiences validate their struggles and remind them that they are not alone—simply hearing the words "I understand" can be profoundly healing, offering a lifeline in what might otherwise feel like an isolating journey.

Beyond traditional therapy, alternative methods of healing can also play a crucial role. Engaging with nature—through walks, hiking, or simply sitting in a quiet outdoor space—has a grounding effect that helps reconnect women with their bodies and the world around them. Retreats designed for survivors of trauma offer an opportunity to step away from daily stresses and focus entirely on self-care and recovery. Creative outlets such as journaling, painting, or dance can allow women to express emotions that words alone cannot capture, providing a channel for release and understanding.

A crucial element of healing is building a support system. While self-reliance is a strength, no one should face the weight of trauma alone. Identifying individuals who can provide genuine support—whether through listening, encouragement, or simply being present—can make an enormous difference. These connections act as anchors during moments of vulnerability, reminding women that they are seen, valued, and cared for. Even a single supportive relationship can serve as a foundation for rebuilding trust and finding stability.

Healing also involves reclaiming control over one's life. Trauma often strips women of their sense of agency, leaving them feeling powerless and adrift. Overcoming this requires deliberate action—setting boundaries, making decisions that prioritize self-care, and finding ways to regain a sense of autonomy. Small, achievable goals can create a sense of momentum, reinforcing the idea that progress, no matter how incremental, is still progress.

Perhaps one of the most transformative steps in healing is finding a sense of purpose beyond the trauma. Whether it's through helping others who have faced similar challenges, pursuing passions that were once abandoned, or simply rediscovering joy in everyday moments, this process allows women to move from merely surviving to truly living.

It's about creating a life that is not defined by the trauma but shaped by the strength and resilience gained in its aftermath.

Healing is not about erasing the past—it's about learning to live with it, to integrate the experiences into a narrative that acknowledges pain while celebrating growth.

It's a journey that requires patience, self-compassion, and an openness to new possibilities. For many women, it is the act of overcoming that redefines who they are, turning the story of trauma into one of triumph and transformation.

Chapter 11
Fear Ain't the Boss of Me

Fear used to drive my life. Fear of judgment. Fear of failure. Fear of being alone. But the scariest part? Fear of being fully seen.

I had walked through so many shadows—divorce, abuse, health scares, betrayal.

But it wasn't until my son and my grandson smiled at me with those innocent eyes that I realized: I wanted to live free. Unapologetically. Boldly.

Fear still knocks sometimes. It whispers that I'm too old, too damaged, too late. But I've stopped answering the door. Because I've already walked through fire. And I've come out not just alive—but powerful.

Now I walk into rooms knowing I belong. I say what I mean. I love loudly. I don't dim my light anymore. Not for comfort. Not for culture. Not for anyone.

I've got dreams to chase—legacies to build. And fear? She can watch from the sidelines because of this story. It's mine now.

"Feel the fear and do it anyway."

— Susan Jeffers.

Fear is universal. It does not discriminate or choose its moments based on convenience. Instead, it comes uninvited, often at times when we least expect it, catching us off guard and forcing us to confront our vulnerabilities.

To acknowledge fear is not to admit defeat—it's a declaration of humanity. We all experience moments of weakness, times when life feels heavier than we can manage, and our courage seems to falter. These moments do not define us; rather, how we respond to them does.

For a long time, I struggled with admitting my own fears. I wore a mask of confidence that allowed me to walk into any room with my head held high, projecting an air of composure and control. Beneath that exterior, however, fear often lingered. It whispered doubts, played on insecurities, and made me question my ability to navigate the world. I thought admitting to these feelings would make me appear weak or incapable, and so I kept them buried.

But fear and vulnerability are not signs of weakness—they are reminders of our humanity. They expose our struggles, yes, but they also highlight our resilience. To admit fear is to open the door to growth, to allow ourselves the space to process and overcome. It is a powerful act of self-compassion to say, "I am afraid," because it also leaves room for the next sentence: "But I will face it."

Fear, at its core, is an inevitable part of life. It is present in the moments of uncertainty, the times we step into the unknown, and the transitions that shape who we are.

It is a teacher, albeit an unwelcome one, pushing us to confront what we may not want to see, but we must do so if we are to move forward. By embracing these moments of vulnerability, we allow ourselves to grow—not in spite of our fears but because of them.

For as long as I can remember, I've carried a fear of not fitting in. It didn't matter where I was—school, work, social settings—I often felt like the outsider, the black sheep in a room full of people who seemed to belong. On the surface, I exuded confidence. I would walk into a space with my head held high, projecting a sense of assurance and poise. Yet, beneath that exterior was an ever-present fear of being different, of not being understood or accepted.

This fear only deepened when I was diagnosed with Lupus. Suddenly, I wasn't just the woman who didn't quite fit in; I became the woman with the condition that others couldn't see, but that consumed me entirely.

Lupus is an illness that operates in silence, leaving no visible scars for others to recognize but wreaking havoc on the body and soul. People would often say, "But you don't look sick," not understanding that beneath the surface, I was fighting a war they couldn't see. The swollen joints, the aching muscles, the days spent unable to move from bed—all of it hidden behind the mask I had learned to wear so well.

Lupus's unpredictability brought about its own set of fears. It stripped me of the ability to plan without hesitation, as every day became a question mark. Would I wake up feeling strong enough to leave the house, or would I collapse under the weight of fatigue? Would I manage to keep my commitments, or would the pain leave me immobilized?

These uncertainties chipped away at my sense of self and heightened my fear of being judged or misunderstood.

Social isolation became an almost inevitable consequence. There were times I made plans, bought tickets to events, and even dressed up, only to cancel at the last minute because my body wouldn't cooperate. I feared the judgment of others, the unspoken assumption that I was flaky or unreliable.

Over time, this fear of disappointing others became a fear of engaging altogether, pushing me further into isolation.

And yet, Lupus brought a new dimension to my identity, one I had no choice but to confront. It forced me to grapple with the fear of not just being different but being seen as weak or incapable. I found myself hiding the realities of my illness, unwilling to show the moments when I fell to the floor because my body gave out or the mornings when I sat in my car, unable to drive because the fatigue was too great. I feared that revealing these truths would alienate me further, leaving me even more isolated in a world where I already felt like an outsider.

This fear of not fitting in, compounded by the physical and emotional toll of Lupus, created a cycle of self-doubt and withdrawal. It was as though I was constantly trying to navigate two worlds: the one where I pretended everything was fine and the one where I faced the full reality of my illness. Reconciling these two worlds felt impossible at times, leaving me in a state of limbo—present but not fully engaged, visible but unseen.

Despite the challenges, this fear taught me something invaluable: the importance of honesty, both with myself and with others. I began to see that true belonging doesn't come from fitting in but from embracing who you are, even when that means standing apart. It's a lesson I'm still learning, but with every step, I move closer to understanding that being different doesn't diminish my value—it defines my strength.

In the midst of all my fears and struggles, the turning point came not from within but from the unwavering love and support of my son and grandson. They became the anchors that grounded me when I felt adrift, the light that guided me through the darkest moments of my life. Their presence constantly reminded me why I needed to keep pushing forward, even when everything in me wanted to give up.

My son has always been a source of strength for me. He grew up seeing me as his Superwoman, the mother who could handle anything life threw her way.

But as life wore me down—the trauma, the Lupus diagnosis, and the fear of not fitting in—I began to question whether I could live up to the image he held of me. It was during one of our heartfelt conversations that I finally allowed myself to be vulnerable with him, admitting that even Superwoman has moments when she can't wear the cape.

That conversation was transformative. In his eyes, my moments of weakness didn't make me any less of a hero; they made me human. He reminded me that strength isn't about being invincible—it's about showing up, even when it's hard. Through him, I began to see that I didn't have to pretend to be unbreakable to be a good mother. It was okay to let him see my struggles, to show him that even in the face of fear and pain, I was still fighting.

Then came my grandson, a gift I hadn't anticipated but one that changed everything. From the moment he was born, he brought a new kind of joy into my life, a joy that reignited a fire within me. Holding him for the first time, I felt an overwhelming sense of purpose. He was a living reminder that life moves forward and that there is always something worth fighting for, no matter how heavy the burden.

My grandson gave me the push I needed to make changes. I wanted to be someone he could look up to, someone who could show him what resilience and love look like. His laughter, his curiosity, and the pure innocence in his eyes reminded me that life is not just about enduring but about finding moments of beauty and connection even amidst the chaos.

It was their love that made me realize I couldn't continue down the path of self-isolation and fear. They gave me the strength to face my reality head-on, to stop hiding my illness, and to embrace the life I still had. Through them, I began to rebuild myself—not as the person I used to be, but as someone stronger, wiser, and more intentional.

Their influence taught me that fear and vulnerability don't have to define you. They can become the catalysts for growth and transformation with love and support.

My son and grandson reminded me that I am still a source of strength, not despite my struggles but because of them. They showed me that even in my weakest moments, I have the power to rise and keep moving forward.

Reclaiming my fearless self was not an instant transformation but a gradual process—a series of deliberate choices and small victories that allowed me to step back into the confidence and boldness I once embodied. Fear had taken its toll on me, leaving me hesitant, guarded, and unsure of my place in the world. Yet, the determination to live fully and embrace life on my own terms became stronger with every step forward.

There was a time when I approached life without hesitation, taking on challenges with the belief that I could conquer anything. I was unafraid of failure or judgment, driven by an innate confidence that fueled my ambitions. But life has a way of humbling even the most fearless among us. The trauma, the Lupus diagnosis, and the weight of societal expectations chipped away at my sense of self, leaving me uncertain and cautious where I had once been bold.

It was through writing this book, among other endeavors, that I began to reclaim that part of myself. Putting my experiences into words forced me to confront my fears and doubts head-on. It reminded me of my strength, of all the battles I had already fought and survived. Each word became an act of defiance, a declaration that fear would no longer dictate the narrative of my life.

Writing gave me back my voice, a voice I had silenced for far too long.

I also took deliberate steps to rebuild my confidence in everyday life. I began to show up for myself in ways I hadn't before—whether it was pursuing personal goals, expanding my business, or simply allowing myself to be seen as I truly was. No more hiding behind the fear of not fitting in or of being judged for my illness. I realized that my experiences, even the painful ones, were a testament to my resilience and a source of inspiration for others.

Living boldly meant embracing the fullness of who I am, scars and all. It meant recognizing that fear is not the absence of courage but the companion of it. I started to take risks again, to believe in my abilities, and to trust in the strength that had carried me through some of the darkest moments of my life. Slowly, I began to see the fearless version of myself reemerge—not as the person I once was but as someone transformed by the journey.

The love and support of my son and grandson played a pivotal role in this transformation.

They reminded me that I was still capable of greatness and had a purpose and a legacy to create. Their faith in me reignited my own belief in myself, giving me the courage to dream again and the determination to make those dreams a reality.

Reclaiming my fearlessness has been about more than just overcoming the challenges I've faced; it's been about redefining what it means to be strong. It's about standing in my truth, owning my story, and refusing to let fear have the final say.

Today, I live with a renewed sense of purpose, driven not by the need to prove myself to others but by the desire to honor the journey that has brought me here.

To anyone reading this, I want you to know that it's never too late to reclaim your confidence, to find your voice, and to live boldly.

Fear may always linger in the background, but it doesn't have to hold you back. With every step you take, you remind yourself—and the world—that you are so much more than your struggles. You are capable, courageous, and, above all, unstoppable.

Chapter 12
Know Who You Are

There's a freedom that comes from knowing exactly who you are—but there's also a war that's fought to get there.

I knew who I was once. A young girl married at 17, full of light and belief, hoping love would be enough to carry me. But with its hard edges and unfair turns, life tried to strip that knowing from me. The rejection from my first husband's family stung. The side-eyes in congregations, the gossip whispered in religious corners, the lies about my name—all of it chipped away at my identity.

I was told I wasn't enough. Not worthy enough. Not wife enough. Not woman enough. But those were their lies, not my truth.

After the heartbreak of my first marriage, I tried again. This time, I did the work. Financially, I rebuilt. Spiritually, I realigned. Mentally and physically, I found strength. I asked the right questions, did the research, and peeled back the layers. Or so I thought.

Turns out, I wasn't marrying a partner—I was marrying a storybook of lies. The house? Almost gone. The business? Crumbling. The truth? Twisted beyond recognition. His children, his past, his abuse—all hidden behind a polished smile and a desperate need for validation. Once again, I was left questioning the reflection staring back at me in the mirror. But this time, I didn't shatter. I reconstructed.

I gathered the broken pieces of my faith, dignity, and self-worth and started laying them down like bricks—building something new, something stronger. It wasn't about going back to who I was before the pain. It was about becoming someone even the pain couldn't destroy.

"When you've been broken apart, you don't put yourself back the same way—you redesign. You rise wiser."

Knowing who you are means knowing where you deserve to be—and, just as importantly, where you don't.

After all I'd endured, I found myself withdrawing. When you've survived what others wouldn't even recognize in fiction, you start to guard your spirit like a sacred temple. It's not fear—it's discernment. I stopped showing up for spaces that didn't deserve my energy. I stopped entering rooms where I had to shrink to fit.

I stopped explaining myself to people who were committed to misunderstanding me. I stopped watering dead plants, hoping they would bloom.

Instead, I sought out rooms that felt like sunlight. Places that lifted me. People who reflected the version of me I'd fought to become. I chose spaces where healing could happen, where my scars weren't taboos but testaments.

The more I aligned with truth, the more I realized that healing isn't always loud—it's sometimes a soft, steady rising. A private revolution is happening in the quiet corners of your soul.

Part of this reclamation was realizing that solitude wasn't punishment—it was peace. I'm a hermit by human design, and now I understand why. I don't run from quiet anymore. I rest in it. I recharge in the stillness, where I can hear my own voice again after a world of noise.

"Sometimes your best company is your own soul whispering, 'You're doing just fine.'"

The silence became my sanctuary. In those undisturbed moments, I met the most honest parts of myself—the ones that weren't performing, pleasing, or proving anything to anyone.

When I step into social spaces, I come as my whole self. I walk in with my head high, my heart open—but my discernment intact. Social intelligence is more than charm or small talk. It's knowing how to hold a room while holding your peace. It's knowing when to speak and when to observe simply.

It's learning to read the energy between words, to recognize when presence is enough and when absence is necessary.

I've learned to be selective with my energy, especially with relationships. Not everyone who smiles at you means well. Some come cloaked in love but carry the poison of manipulation. And the hardest truth of all? Sometimes, those people are family. Sometimes, they're in the pulpit. Sometimes, they share your bed.

But I've stopped asking for others to validate me. I am no longer bending into shapes just to be accepted. I've found freedom in authenticity, and I'm committed to fostering reciprocal, not draining, relationships.

Loyalty is not owed to dysfunction. Love doesn't require self-abandonment. And forgiveness does not mean access.

So, if I can offer anything—if you take nothing else from this chapter—let it be this: Know who you are.

Not who they said you are. Not what trauma tried to convince you to become. Not who you pretended to be to survive.

But who you are.

Know her. Love her. Protect her.

Speak to her gently on the days she forgets. Celebrate her loudly when she rises. Remind her she is not a mistake. She is a miracle.

When you truly know who you are, your boundaries get firmer, your light gets brighter, and your future gets clearer.

"Knowing who you are is the first step to becoming who you're meant to be."

And baby, you were meant to be extraordinary.

Reflection: What parts of yourself have you silenced to survive? What would it look like to reclaim those pieces today?

Reflection (continued): What rooms have you stayed in out of fear, and what would it mean to walk out finally? What truths have you buried beneath politeness or pride? Who would you be without the weight of proving anything?

Prayer:

Dear God,

Remind me of who I truly am. Strip away every label that pain, rejection, or fear has placed on me. Heal the pieces that still ache from the past. Guide me into rooms that honor my spirit. Help me to walk boldly, love wisely, and live authentically. And when I forget my worth, whisper it back to me. Amen.

And if I stumble, if I fall into old wounds or familiar patterns, lift me gently. Remind me that healing is not linear—and becoming takes time. Amen.

Chapter 13
Being on Your Own

May I start by saying that women have always had to do it all?

We've carried families, built businesses, dried tears, and wiped our own in silence. Whether it's due to survival, generational cycles, or simply the demands of life, we often find ourselves showing up with a kind of strength that doesn't wait to be asked. And let's be real—it doesn't matter if you're single, married, partnered, or surrounded by people. You can have a man in the house and still feel alone in the doing, still be the one holding it all together.

That kind of weight doesn't care about your relationship status. It finds you because you're capable and stays because you never complain.

When I chose to raise my son on my own, I knew what came with it. I knew the whispers. The judgments. The uninvited narratives people like to project. But I also knew this—I would show up for him and myself in every way I could. I held myself to a high standard. I didn't need to prove anyone wrong, but I wanted to prove to myself that I could give him a life full of opportunity, joy, and foundation.

I wanted him to see resilience not as a burden but as a birthright. I wanted him to know that love still holds even when stretched thin.

I worked three jobs. I walked for miles, pulling my son in a little green wagon to the train and to the bus, just to drop him off at my parents before heading to work. And then I'd do it all over again in reverse. I tried to go to school at night. One friend—just one—made the difference. She lent me her car, gave me rides, and never made me feel like I was a burden. She knew what I was going through because she was going through it, too.

She didn't just help, she held space. Sometimes, that's all we need: someone who sees us without flinching.

One boss considered me. He saw more than a struggling young mom. He saw potential. His wife and sister joined in to support me. They helped me land a job with an NFL team. Yes, from bus rides and green wagons to boardrooms and stadium seats. They lifted me when others couldn't because they had the capacity and the insight. They had been where I wanted to go, and they believed in my journey.

And their belief wasn't performative; it was actionable. They didn't just say, "You can do it." They made sure I had the tools to try.

It wasn't glamorous. It wasn't easy. But it was mine.

"Being on your own doesn't mean being without power. Sometimes, it's where your power is forged."

Because fire doesn't just burn—it also refines. And I was being refined by every setback, every mile, every unanswered prayer.

Looking back, the only thing I would change is this: never let your connections die. Never shrink yourself. Never assume you don't belong. I started to feel like maybe I wasn't meant to walk in certain rooms, but I was. I was invited. I was equipped. I belonged.

But no one tells you that belonging is something you sometimes have to claim before it's handed to you. Confidence had to be built in silence before it could be spoken aloud.

I never wanted to be a statistic, a young Black single mother with no aspirations. And truthfully, I didn't come from destruction. My home wasn't broken, but it was demanding. I was raised on discipline, expectations, and the sacred commandment: *"You must be better than us. You must do more."*

That pressure molded me, but it also exhausted me. I had to learn that worth isn't always measured in performance. It's also in the presence.

Being on my own was far from romantic. It was no fairy tale, no breezy walk down golden streets. It was grit, it was fatigue; the dozen doubted it. It was looking in the mirror, wondering if I'd lost myself under the weight of responsibility.

It was building dreams in the margins of exhaustion. It was showing up anyway, on the days when joy felt like a language I no longer spoke.

I faced obstacles many wouldn't believe. There were courts that treated me like a threat, and religion that boxed me in and boxed me out.

There were silent battles with depression, and loud accusations from people who thought my tears meant instability. They didn't understand that crying was my rebellion. My release. My protest. Because I did have a voice, it was just cracking from all the shouting it had to do to be heard.

They're the body's way of saying, 'I survived that too.'

"Your tears are not weakness; they're evidence that your soul still feels and still fights."

To the woman reading this, here's what I want you to know about overcoming:

You don't need permission to heal. You don't need validation to rise. You don't have to carry shame for choosing yourself.

You are allowed to disappoint people who expect you to suffer silently. You are allowed to be the version of yourself they never prepared for.

Find your rhythm. Maybe it's three jobs, maybe it's school at night, maybe it's rest. Don't compare your path to anyone else's. Ask for help when you need it. Cherish the friends who show up. Keep every number, every business card, every email. Your future might depend on a past connection you almost forgot.

When you feel overlooked, remember that seeds are buried before they bloom. Your time is not running out—it's taking root.

Get honest about your pain. Cry if you need to. But don't stay silent. Your story deserves a voice, and your life deserves more than survival. It deserves fullness. You were not born just to endure, you were born to embody joy, even if you had to fight for it first.

Being on your own is not a flaw. It's not a punishment. It's a proving ground—a sacred space where the strongest version of you can be born.

"The world will tell you being alone means lack. But being on your own? It just means the story is yours to write."

And trust me, you're holding the pen with power now. Write a narrative that even the past can't undo. Let your next chapter echo with resilience, not regret.

Reflection…

In what areas of your life have you doubted your strength? What stories have you told yourself that you're ready to rewrite?

What would shift if you believed that strength isn't in pretending but in persevering with tenderness? What part of your story still needs to be forgiven by you?

Optional Prayer

God,

In the moments when I feel like I'm carrying the world alone,

Remind me that You walk with me.

Bless my feet for the journeys they've taken,

And bless my heart for the courage it took to walk them.

Help me to see that being on my own isn't abandonment—it's an assignment.

One where I learn to trust, to grow, and to rise. Amen.

And when I forget why I started, steady me. When I question if I'm enough, quiet my doubt, help me finish the climb with faith in my hands and peace in my bones. Amen.

Chapter 14
Self-Love

"When you choose yourself, you teach the world how to treat you."

Self-love isn't selfish. It's survival. It's sacred. It's the divine act of remembering who you were before the world told you otherwise.

And baby, it's time to remember.

It's time to return to the parts of you that never needed to beg, to prove, or to perform.

We weren't born begging for worth. Somewhere along the way, the world taught us to question ourselves. It taught us that being strong meant being silent. That choosing ourselves meant abandoning others. That love was a reward for suffering well. But let me remind you—you do not have to earn love through pain.

You do not have to bleed to be worthy of belonging. You do not have to lose yourself to be loved by others.

We've spent too long overextending for others while ignoring the girl inside us who was screaming for permission just to be.

Permission to be soft.

To be seen.

To stop carrying what was never hers.

Choosing Yourself: The Sacred Rebellion

There comes a moment.

A hush.

A break.

A breath.

When you whisper to yourself, *"I can't do this like this anymore."*

That whisper is holy. It's the start of your return.

It's the moment where exhaustion meets awakening. Where pretending finally breaks under the weight of truth.

Choosing yourself is not loud. It's not petty. It's not for show. It's the quiet courage, the brave decision to love yourself out of survival mode.

To stop fighting for a seat at tables you built.

To stop begging people to treat you like you matter.

It's not abandonment. It's alignment.

It's not selfishness. It's stewardship.

It's not giving up. It's giving in—to the version of you that's been waiting to breathe.

To the woman, you were before shrinking became your second language.

The Cost of Self-Abandonment

When you don't choose yourself, your body remembers.

The headaches. The panic attacks. The tears that show up uninvited. The silence that feels like slow suffocation.

That's not peace—that's your soul waving the white flag.

That's your body begging you to listen, begging you to stop trading your well-being for approval.

You perform for approval and call it strength.

You stay in places you've outgrown because the unknown feels riskier than the pain you've come to expect.

But you were not created to shrink.

Not for a job.

Not for a man.

Not for a title.

Not for your mama's expectations or the church's approval.

Let me say this loud—

You are not required to set yourself on fire to keep other people warm.

You are not a container for everyone else's comfort while yours sits empty.

How to Choose You—For Real?

Choosing yourself looks like leaving the text unread.

Not showing up just to be polite. Saying *"no"* without a paragraph of apology.

It looks like:

- Resting without guilt.
- Celebrating your small wins.
- Crying without calling yourself weak.
- Asking for help.
- Saying, “I matter, even if no one else claps.”
- Letting go of roles that only survive when you disappear in them.

Start with honesty. Sit with yourself and ask:

- What have I been tolerating?
- Where have I been betraying myself?
- Whose voice is in my head—and should it be?
- What do I actually want?

And then listen. Not to the noise.

But to the knowing. She knows.

Loving Yourself in the Daily

Here’s what loving you looks like on a regular Tuesday:

1. Speak Life

Affirm yourself like your life depends on it—because it does.

“I deserve softness.”

"I don't owe hustle my health."

"I am worthy of love that doesn't hurt."

"My boundaries are holy."

2. Guard Your Peace

Everyone doesn't deserve access. That's not shade. That's wisdom.

Your peace is too expensive to rent out for cheap validation.

3. Honor Your Journey

You don't have to be healed to be worthy. Every step matters—even the shaky ones.

Even the ones no one claps for.

4. Reparent the Little Girl Inside

Give her rest. Give her joy. Give her gentleness. Speak to her like she's sacred—because she is.

She's still listening. She still believes you'll choose her one day. Let that day be today.

5. Let Yourself Receive

You don't always have to be the giver.

You don't always have to be the strong one.

Being held is healing, too.

And sometimes the bravest thing you'll ever do is say, "I need support."

Unlearning the Lies

You were told:

- That your needs were too much.
- That rest was laziness.
- That emotions were weaknesses.
- That love required pain.

All lies.

The truth?

You are not a burden.

You are a blessing.

You are not unworthy.

You are unmatched.

You are not too much. You are just enough for the right space, the right people, and the right life.

And if no one told you lately:

You're doing better than you think. And you deserve joy without explanation.

Final Words

There is no award for self-sacrifice.

There is no trophy for carrying everyone else while you crumble.

There is only this moment. And the next one.

And the one after that. All asking you to come home to yourself.

So, show up. Speak kindly. Take up space.

Choose you—again and again—until you no longer flinch when love comes with your name on it.

You don't need permission.

You've had it all along.

Reflection

- Where did you learn that loving yourself was conditional?
- What relationships have required you to abandon yourself?
- What new belief are you ready to embrace about your worth?
- What would change if you treated yourself like someone you love?

- What would your life look like if you truly believed you were enough—even when you're resting, even when you're healing?

Optional Prayer

God,

When I forget who I am, remind me. When I feel unworthy, remind me that You made me worthy. When I question if I matter, whisper it louder than the noise of this world. Help me come home to myself again.

To love what You created. To choose myself not just in theory, but in truth. Amen. And when I doubt my softness, show me that even tenderness can be strength. Teach me to trust my reflection again. Amen.

Affirmation

I will not shrink. I will not settle. I will not wait. I choose me—fully, fiercely, and finally.

And that choice? It changes everything.

Chapter 15
The Impact of Emotionally Unintelligent People

"You are not responsible for someone else's inability to love, listen, or grow."

Let's talk about the unspoken weight—the one that doesn't come from your own trauma, but from absorbing everyone else's. The weight of being in spaces where emotional immaturity is the norm, and emotional intelligence is seen as a weakness. The weight of trying to be the bridge in relationships where no one else is willing to build.

You know the people I'm talking about.

The ones who dismiss your feelings.

The ones who weaponize your vulnerability.

The ones who can't apologize, can't reflect, and sure as hell can't grow.

They hurt you and then blame you for bleeding. They cross your boundaries and then call you "too sensitive."

They disrespect you, and when you respond, they flip the script and suddenly *you're* the problem.

And worse—sometimes, we grow up with these people. Sometimes we call them family, or mentors, or even partners.

When Disrespect Becomes Familiar

Let's get real. If you grew up with emotionally stunted parents, toxic siblings, or passive-aggressive family members, you may have normalized dysfunction. You learned to regulate *them* before you even knew how to regulate *yourself*.

You became the fixer. The peacekeeper. The one who swallowed her voice to avoid conflict.

You knew how to read a room before you learned how to read a book. Because survival made you emotionally hyperaware. You became fluent in tension. Comfortable in chaos. Trained in walking on eggshells.

But the catch? That same emotional intelligence became your prison. Emotionally unintelligent people thrive in spaces where no one calls them out. They're allergic to accountability but addicted to control.

The Blame Game: Their Disrespect, Your Reaction

Let me be clear: emotionally unintelligent people hate accountability.

So when you call out their mess, they don't reflect—they deflect.

You say, "That hurt me."

They say, "You're too sensitive."

You say, "That crossed a line."

They say, "You're always so dramatic."

You try to protect your peace, and suddenly *you're* the villain.

You become the scapegoat because they can't sit with their own shame.

This is emotional manipulation. It's gaslighting.

And it's designed to keep you in a loop where you're always the one apologizing for having basic emotional needs.

It's exhausting.

It's unfair.

And it's **not your fault.**

Growing Up With Emotional Chaos

Some of us didn't just encounter emotionally unintelligent people—we were *raised* by them.

Parents who demanded perfection but offered no empathy. Siblings who competed instead of connected.

Caregivers who saw emotions as rebellion instead of a cry for help.

You may have grown up in a home where:

- Love was conditional.
- Silence was safer than honesty.
- "I'm sorry" was never modeled.

- Vulnerability was mocked.

And now?

- You flinch at kindness.
- You over-explain yourself.
- You apologize for existing.
- You feel guilty when you're finally treated with respect.

Let me tell you something that may shift your whole soul:

That wasn't love. That was control dressed up in obligation.

That was survival, not safety. That was performance, not partnership.

And now you're left unpacking bags that weren't even yours to carry.

The Danger of Normalizing Dysfunction

The biggest danger of emotionally unintelligent people is not just the damage they do—but the damage they convince *you* to do to yourself.

They teach you:

- To silence your truth.
- To accept less.
- To stay small.

But you weren't created to be a doormat.

You weren't designed to constantly explain yourself to people committed to misunderstanding you. You were made for connection, not correction.

You were made for depth, not damage.

Emotionally unintelligent people will keep you in cycles of pain, not because they're evil—but because they're emotionally unequipped.

And it is not your job to raise them.

Not your duty to fix them. Not your calling to bleed for their comfort.

Spotting Emotional Immaturity in Real Time

Let's make this plain. Here's how you spot emotionally immature folks:

- They interrupt when you speak.
- They mock or dismiss your feelings.
- They shut down or lash out instead of engaging.
- They blame everyone else, always.
- They never initiate repair after conflict.
- They make your boundaries about their comfort.

They demand grace but offer none.

They expect loyalty but show inconsistency.

Sometimes they're loud.

Sometimes they're subtle.

But they always make you question your sanity.

Not anymore. Because now, you see the game—and you no longer have to play it.

What to Do With What You Know

Now that you see it, what do you do?

1. Set boundaries like your peace depends on it—because it does.

It's okay to love someone and not let them destroy you. You're allowed to protect yourself from people you still care about.

2. Stop explaining your worth.

If someone needs a thesis to respect your basic needs, they're not ready.

You don't need to earn dignity.

You were born with it.

3. Heal loudly.

Let them call you dramatic.

Let them say you changed. You're allowed to grow past the version of you that tolerated disrespect. Healing will offend the people who benefited from your brokenness.

4. Reclaim your voice.

You were not born to whisper. You were not born to pacify people who refuse to grow.

5. Get support.

Therapy. Community. Prayer. Journaling.

You don't have to heal in isolation.

Isolation may have protected you—but connection will restore you.

Final Truths

Emotionally unintelligent people will always try to dim your light—It helps them ignore their own darkness. But your healing isn't a threat.It's a mirror.

You don't need to fight them.

You don't need to prove anything.

You don't need to argue to be understood.

You just need to protect your peace like it's sacred—Because it is.

You're not too sensitive.

You're emotionally intelligent in a world that often isn't.

And that, my love, is your superpower.

Reflection Prompts

- Where in your life have you been gaslit into silence?
- What family dynamics still haunt your emotional responses today?
- Who do you need distance from to breathe fully again?
- What boundary are you ready to finally set?
- What part of your voice are you reclaiming now—and who taught you to silence it in the first place?

Optional Prayer

God,

Help me to see clearly what clouds my peace.

Give me the courage to walk away from cycles that shrink me. Remind me that my emotions are not too much—they are mine, and they are holy. When I feel guilty for choosing myself, remind me that healing is not betrayal.

Help me forgive the emotionally immature—not for their sake, but for mine. Because I'm ready to be free. Amen. And if I ever start to doubt what I know, speak truth back into me. Remind me that clarity is a gift—and I don't have to give it back. Amen.

Chapter 16
Identifying Conditioning

"Not everything you were taught is truth—some of it was survival wrapped in fear."

Let's talk about the invisible chains. The rules we live by that no longer serve us. The unspoken beliefs we carry that were never ours to begin with.

This chapter is about identifying conditioning—the inherited patterns, toxic traditions, and subconscious stories we've been running on autopilot since childhood.

The stories that taught us how to survive—but never how to thrive.

See, many of us are living lives that were programmed—not chosen.

We were conditioned to put others first.

To stay small.

To endure instead of evolve.

To make ourselves palatable instead of powerful.

And here's the kicker—we didn't even realize it was happening. Because it was called "love." Because it came dressed as tradition. Because we didn't know we had a choice.

What Is Conditioning, Really?

Conditioning is what happens when someone else's limitations become your life script.

It's the voice in your head that says:

- "Don't speak unless spoken to."
- "People will think you're full of yourself."
- "That's not for people like us."
- "You're too much."

It's generational.

It's cultural.

It's religious.

It's familial.

It's the stuff we don't even question because it came from people we loved, respected, or feared.

But love doesn't make it right. Respect doesn't equal truth. Tradition doesn't equal wisdom.

And if it's keeping you bound, it's time to break it.

The Silent Hand of Influence

Maybe you were taught to dim your light so others could shine. Maybe you were told emotions were a weakness.

Maybe you grew up hearing that being a good woman meant being quiet, agreeable, accommodating—even when it broke you.

This isn't about blame. It's about awareness.

Because healing doesn't start with anger—it starts with honesty.

If we don't name it, we'll repeat it. And we'll pass it on to our children, our partners, our businesses, and ourselves.

Unhealed conditioning becomes inherited pain.

And you were not born to pass on what you were called to release.

Spotting the Invisible Barriers

Conditioning shows up in sneaky ways:

- You feel guilty for resting.
- You over-explain your "no."
- You assume success has to come with struggle.
- You shrink in rooms where you should shine.
- You mistake self-neglect for humility.

These aren't personality traits. They're inherited rules. Invisible scripts running your life like background apps draining your battery.

To heal, you must begin to notice them.

Ask yourself:

- Who taught me this?
- Why do I believe it?

- Is it serving me now?
- Would I want my daughter to believe this?

Because if the answer is no—it's time to release it.

It's time to write your own script. One built on truth, not fear.

Breaking Free: The Undoing

Unlearning takes work. But it's sacred work.

You don't just delete a belief like a bad email.

You untrain your brain.

You unteach the fear.

You return to the truth.

That means:

- Replacing shame with curiosity.
- Rewriting "should" with truth.
- Practicing the opposite of what you were taught, even when it feels wrong.
- Sitting in the discomfort until it becomes freedom.

If you were raised in scarcity, practicing abundance will feel irresponsible at first.

If you were raised in silence, using your voice will feel loud.

If you were raised on performance, choosing peace will make you feel lazy.

That's not fear. That's freedom waking up.

That's your nervous system adjusting to liberation.

A Scenario: When the Fog Lifts

Let me give you an example:

She was raised to believe women should stay married "no matter what."

That divorce was a failure.

That independence was selfish.

Her mother did it. Her grandmother did it.

Even when the love was gone.

Even when the bruises showed.

She grew up repeating the cycle. Until one day, she realized that her silence was killing her.

She left. And at first, she felt like she was betraying her lineage.

But she wasn't.

She was redeeming it. She was rewriting the legacy in real time.

Now she's teaching her daughter that leaving isn't failure—it's freedom. That joy isn't selfish—it's necessary.

That sacrifice without self-preservation isn't love—it's martyrdom.

That's how we break chains. One choice at a time.

One truth at a time. One brave “no more” at a time.

Why It’s Hard to Unlearn?

Conditioning isn’t just mental—it’s emotional. It comes with:

- Guilt (“I’m dishonoring my family.”)
- Fear (“What will they think?”)
- Shame (“Who do I think I am?”)

But let me ask you:

- Who benefits from you staying small?
- Who loses when you finally walk in truth?

Sometimes the fear isn’t about failing—it’s about no longer being who they expected you to be. It’s about losing the identity you wore to survive.

But you weren’t born to live their dreams.

You were born to rise. You were born to break the silence, not be buried by it.

New Scripts, New Life

Here’s how you begin to rewrite the script:

- Catch the thought. Name the conditioning.
- Challenge it. Ask if it’s even true.
- Replace it. Use affirmations, truth, and action.

- Be patient with your mind while it adjusts to a new truth.

Examples:

Old Script: “I can’t charge that much. No one will pay.”

New Script: “My work is valuable and I set prices based on worth, not fear.”

***

Old Script: “I can’t speak up—they’ll think I’m difficult.”

New Script: “I honor my voice and speak with truth and clarity.”

***

Old Script: “I need to make everyone happy to be loved.”

New Script: “My value isn’t based on how well I perform for others.”

Every time you choose the new script, you weaken the old one. Every time you challenge a lie, you reclaim a part of yourself.

This is how freedom builds.

This is how legacy changes.

Final Words

Unlearning isn't betrayal.

It's returning—to the *you* that existed before fear entered the room. To the you who knew she was enough before the world told her otherwise.

You have permission to:

- Leave what's familiar.
- Outgrow what they called tradition.
- Question everything.

You are not your upbringing.

You are not your trauma.

You are not the container they tried to fit you in.

You are expansion.

You are reclamation.

You are reprogramming yourself for freedom.

And that's holy. That's sacred. That's necessary.

Reflection Prompts

- What beliefs were you taught that you no longer align with?
- Where in your life do you still feel the need to "earn" love, rest, or peace?
- Who are you when no one else is watching?

- What would your life look like if you unlearned fear?
- What script are you ready to write for yourself from a place of truth—not tradition?

Optional Prayer

God,

Help me to see what no longer belongs. Shine light on the beliefs that keep me stuck.

Give me the courage to question, to release, and to rewrite. Help me trade false stories for sacred truth. May I honor my lineage without repeating its wounds. And may my healing ripple through generations.

Amen.

And when I forget who I'm becoming, remind me of who I was before the world taught me to hide.

Amen.

Chapter 17
Suicidal Idealization

"Some days survival doesn't feel noble—it feels like barely breathing. But even then, breath is a miracle."

There are certain conversations we tend to avoid—the ones that live in the shadows. We dance around them with metaphors and euphemisms, trying to keep everything polished and digestible.

This chapter is about what happens when the world gets too heavy to carry. When the noise outside becomes too loud, and the silence inside becomes deafening. When you wake up, you wonder not if you'll make it but if you even want to.

This isn't about glorifying pain or dramatizing despair. It's about naming an experience many have lived through, even if they've never said the words out loud. Suicidal idealization doesn't always look the way people expect. It's not always screaming in pain or collapsing in a puddle of tears. More often, it's quiet. It wears a mask. It goes to work. It shows up to brunch. It cracks jokes. It keeps everything running—until it doesn't.

Sometimes, suicidal thoughts don't come because you want to die. They come because you're exhausted from living in pain.

My Story: The Ninth Grade

I was just 14 when I reached my breaking point. In the ninth grade, while life at home felt structured, safe, and filled with love, everything outside those four walls felt like a battlefield. At school, I became the target of other people's insecurities, picked on daily for reasons that had nothing to do with my character and everything to do with their own pain.

I didn't fit in. I didn't come from struggle. I dressed well, smiled often, and spoke with confidence. I was smart, ambitious, and took pride in how I carried myself. But those very traits—my light—seemed to offend the world around me. Girls in my school targeted me for everything I didn't apologize for. They said I had too much. That I acted like I was better. They mocked my colored contacts, my grades, my joy.

Every encounter chipped away at my sense of self. I began to shrink, not because I believed what they said, but because I didn't have the tools to fight it. It was like I was living in two worlds: one where I was loved and supported, and another where I was constantly being punished for simply existing.

Eventually, the darkness became too loud to ignore. I tried to end my life. I was hospitalized. I remember drinking charcoal to remove the toxins from my system, staring at the ceiling while wondering how I'd gotten there. I wasn't even old enough to drive, but I had already reached a point where staying alive felt like too much.

But something changed that year. I started therapy. For the first time, I had a space where I could speak freely, without judgment, where I could be both soft and strong. Where someone looked me in the eye and said, "You don't have to carry all of this alone."

Therapy became more than treatment—it became my lifeline. From that day forward, I made a promise to myself: I would never be ashamed of needing help. I would choose support over silence. I would reach for tools instead of pretending to be okay.

The Allure of Escape

One of the hardest things to admit is that suicidal thoughts don't always feel terrifying. Sometimes, they masquerade as peace. They come not with screams but with sighs. They whisper that disappearing would be easier. That letting go would mean rest. That not being here would be the only way to stop the ache you can't name.

This is why suicidal idealization can be so dangerous—it convinces you that it's not about death, but about finally feeling free. In those moments, the idea of not existing doesn't feel like destruction. It feels like a break. A moment of silence. A full stop in a world that won't let you pause.

But the truth is, these thoughts are not signs that you're ungrateful or weak. They are signals. They point to the depth of your exhaustion, your overwhelm, your pain. They are the language of a nervous system that's been in survival mode for too long.

Your soul isn't giving up. It's asking for a different way forward. It's pleading for relief in the only language it knows.

Breaking the Silence

Too often, people suffer in silence because they believe their pain is an inconvenience. They're afraid of being seen as unstable, ungrateful, or attention-seeking. But pain doesn't require a permission slip. You don't have to explain why you're hurting to be worthy of help. You don't have to prove your suffering for it to be valid.

If you've been carrying suicidal thoughts, let this be your reminder: you are not broken. You are not dramatic. You are not selfish. You are a human being navigating a world that can be unspeakably heavy. If you feel like you've reached your limit, that doesn't mean you're weak—it means you've been strong for too long without rest.

We need to normalize saying, *"I'm not okay."* We need to hold space for that truth without panic or platitudes because healing begins when honesty enters the room.

When Despair Turns to Defiance

Something strange can happen when you've been dancing with death in your mind: you stop fearing consequences. You start doing the things you once thought were impossible, not out of empowerment, but out of exhaustion. You quit the job. You cut off the toxic family.

You travel alone. You tell your truth, even if it shakes the room.

These moments of defiance, these sudden shifts, aren't always reckless. Sometimes, they're your soul saying, *"If I'm going to live, I have to do it differently."* These can be turning points.

What if we chose ourselves before the breakdown? What if we stopped waiting until we were at the edge to honor our needs, speak our truth, and make bold changes?

If You've Thought About the End

If you've been there, if you've stood in front of the mirror wondering if it's worth continuing, I want you to know this: your presence still matters. Your pain hasn't disqualified you. The fact that you're still here means there's more for you.

There is a version of you that has not been fully realized. A version that laughs deeply, loves wholly, and restores gently. That version is not a fantasy. She is waiting. Trust me, she's worth holding on for.

Don't wait to feel ready. Just stay. One more moment. One more breath. One more sunrise. You never know what the next day might bring.

What Healing Can Look Like?

Healing is often quieter than people think. It's not always about massive breakthroughs or big transformations.

Sometimes it looks like brushing your teeth after three days in bed. Sometimes it's texting a friend, even if you don't know what to say. Sometimes it's making a therapy appointment, taking your meds. Drinking a glass of water. Going outside for five minutes.

These moments matter. They're proof that even when the pain is loud, your spirit hasn't stopped reaching for light.

You don't have to go from despair to joy overnight. But if you can find one small way to care for yourself today, you're doing something holy.

You Are Not a Burden

Let me say it plainly: your pain is not an inconvenience. Your truth is not too much. You are not a burden to the people who truly see you. Even if no one around you sees that yet, it doesn't mean you're unworthy. It means you haven't found your space. But that space exists. It will come. You deserve to be in it fully.

Your emotions are not a problem to be solved. They're a message to be listened to. You are not attention-seeking—you are connection-starved. You are not dramatic—you are desperate for relief. And you're not alone.

Final Words

If today feels unbearable, that's okay. Let it be what it is, but don't let it decide your future. Pause. Breathe. Ask for help. Let someone in. Life might not feel beautiful right now, but beauty still exists. You are not done being a part of it.

There's more ahead.

More joy.

More clarity.

More belonging.

You haven't lived your best days yet.

You haven't met every part of yourself yet.

There is more.

And you are worth it.

Reflection Prompts

- When did life first feel too heavy to carry?
- What's one reason you've stayed alive so far?
- Who needs to hear your truth?
- What would your healing journey look like if you believed you deserve to live in peace?
- What small act of care can you give yourself today, even if you don't feel like you deserve it yet?

Optional Prayer

God,

When the weight feels unbearable, meet me in the quiet. When I cannot hold myself together, hold me. Speak peace to the noise in my mind.

Let me feel something again—hope, softness, safety. Remind me that I am not beyond healing. That even in this place, You are still near. Help me choose one more breath.

One more hour. One more tomorrow. Not because it's easy, but because I'm worth the effort.

Amen.

And when I forget that truth, whisper it back to me until I believe it again.

Chapter 18
Looking for Parental Reassurance in Romantic Relationships

"If you never received love in the way you needed it, you might spend your life trying to re-create it with people who never had the tools to give it to you."

Not everyone grew up in chaos or overt trauma. For many, the wound wasn't a lack of food, shelter, or basic care, but a lack of emotional presence. It was the absence of softness. Of consistent reassurance. Of being seen without having to perform.

Our caregivers may have done their best, but that doesn't mean they gave us what we needed. Sometimes the damage is so quiet that we don't realize it exists until it starts echoing in our relationships.

What about that unmet emotional hunger? It rarely disappears. Instead, it disguises itself as neediness. As control and as perfectionism. Often, it follows us into adulthood, trailing behind us into the arms of romantic partners. We don't always look for love—we look for what we lack. We tried to collect the comfort we were owed. We often seek it in people who don't know how to give it either.

Attachment Styles: A Blueprint for Love

Attachment theory helps explain the way our childhood experiences shape our adult connections. The emotional patterns we observed, or were starved of, become blueprints. Whether we realize it or not, many of us are following a script we didn't write.

- If your parents were emotionally available, nurturing, and consistent, you likely developed a secure attachment style. You trust love. You expect care.

- If your caregivers were unpredictable, distant, overbearing, or emotionally unavailable, you may have developed anxious, avoidant, or fearful-avoidant attachment patterns. You trust inconsistently. You anticipate loss, even in the presence of love.

These early dynamics don't stay in the past. They resurface in subtle but powerful ways. You might find yourself:

- Constantly seeking reassurance, even after your partner affirms you.
- Feeling abandoned or panicked when they need space.
- Being drawn to people who don't prioritize your emotional needs—because they feel familiar.
- Trying to fix your partner the way you once wished you could fix a parent who didn't know how to love you fully.

You're not broken. You're operating from a pattern. A pattern that once kept you emotionally safe, but now keeps you emotionally stuck.

The Parent Trap in Partnership

This is where things get deep. Often, we don't realize that we're not falling in love—we're falling into roles. Emotional dynamics. Familiar dysfunction. We subconsciously recreate the environments that shaped us because they feel like home, even when they hurt.

We cling to emotionally unavailable people because they remind us of our emotionally distant fathers. We tolerate volatility because it mimics our mother's moods. We confuse anxiety with passion. We chase rejection and call it romance.

It might feel like love, but what we're really doing is reenacting the pain of never being chosen, hoping that someone will choose us this time.

It's not love we're always after—it's resolution. Closure. Correction of the past. But love cannot be forced to fix what only healing can.

My Story: Carrying Legacy Into Love

I was one of the fortunate ones. My parents gave me what so many crave: emotional safety. They made room for my feelings, celebrated my individuality, and structured my life in a way that protected my innocence. Their rules were firm, yes.

As a teenager, I didn't always understand the restrictions. I wanted more freedom, more autonomy. But now, I'm grateful. That structure wasn't about control—it was about covering. It kept me grounded when the world wanted me reckless.

When I married at 17, I entered into another family's way of doing things. I saw their marriage, their values, and their rhythm. It wasn't the same as what I came from, but it gave me perspective. It gave me a second model. I tried to take what was good from my upbringing, their example, and my evolving values, and create something whole.

But here's where the cracks started to show: I became overly attached to the idea of "doing it right." I wasn't just trying to love my partner. I was trying to be someone my family could be proud of. I wanted my relationships to reflect well on me. I wanted validation. Not because I didn't feel loved, but because I felt responsible for proving I had learned how to love "correctly."

That desire wasn't toxic. It was tender. It came from a place of deep love and deep hope. But when we tie our identity to our ability to perform in love, we start asking partners to fill roles they were never meant to play.

The Unfair Ask

It's not your partner's job to reparent you. It's not their job to make up for the emotional losses of your past. But when we're unaware of our wounds, that's exactly what we try to make them do. We place subconscious expectations on them to be more than a partner, to become a healer, a nurturer, a stand-in for the parent who never came through.

You may find yourself:

- Expecting them to prove their love over and over again.
- Interpreting their need for space as abandonment.
- Feeling anxious when they don't respond quickly.
- Needing constant affirmation just to feel secure.

Over time, love becomes a performance. Affection becomes a currency you feel you have to earn. And the relationship begins to feel exhausting, not because either person is bad, but because the expectations are silently crushing the connection.

You cannot experience true intimacy when you're trying to be rescued by your partner. You deserve to be met, not mended.

The Awareness Shift

The first step toward healing this pattern is self-awareness. You have to ask the hard but honest questions:

- Am I looking to my partner to give me what I never received as a child?
- Am I confusing anxiety with connection?
- Do I believe I have to prove myself in order to be loved?

Awareness isn't about blame. It's about freedom. When you begin to name the pattern, you no longer have to be ruled by it. When you shine light on your emotional inheritance, you give yourself the chance to choose something new.

Healing Is Your Job

You may not be able to rewrite your childhood, but you can reparent yourself. You can become the person you once needed—the voice, the presence, the nurturer. You do this by:

- Speaking to yourself with tenderness and patience.
- Creating routines that make you feel safe.
- Setting boundaries that reinforce your value.
- Giving yourself permission to feel without shame.

This is not about blaming your parents or pushing partners away.

It's about reclaiming the responsibility for your healing. When you do that, you begin to show up in relationships whole, not hoping to be completed.

You stop choosing people to fix you, and instead choose people who reflect the healing you've already begun.

A Note on Grief

The healing process may bring up grief you didn't expect. It's not just sadness for what happened—it's mourning what never did.

You may grieve the childhood you deserved but didn't receive. You may cry for the version of yourself who spent years trying to be enough for people who didn't have the capacity to see you.

This grief is not weakness. It's sacred. It's the recognition of your worth. While you may have to feel it fully, you don't have to stay there. You get to move forward, not by forgetting, but by choosing differently.

Grief clears space. It makes room for new stories, new love, new expectations rooted in truth—not pain.

Final Words

Your partner is not your parent.

Your healing is not their responsibility.

But your wholeness?

That is your right.

You deserve love that doesn't come with conditions, confusion, or crisis.

You deserve to be chosen—not because you earned it, but because you're worthy.

And when you begin to love from fullness, not lack, your relationships start to reflect that clarity.

You don't have to keep trying to heal your childhood through your romance.

You can begin again.

You can love differently.

You can be loved well.

Reflection Prompts

- In what ways have you sought parental love in romantic relationships?
- What emotional needs went unmet in your childhood?
- How can you begin meeting those needs for yourself now?
- What would change if you approached love from a place of fullness instead of fear?
- **What qualities do you want to experience in love that your younger self never knew were possible?**

Optional Prayer

God,

Help me to stop looking for my parents in lovers. Teach me how to nurture the child within me. Show me the places I've been seeking healing through people who can't provide it. Give me the strength to break patterns I've carried for too long.

Remind me that I am worthy of love that is consistent, safe, and kind. Let me create a connection from truth, not trauma. And when I forget, bring me back to myself with grace.

Amen.

Chapter 19
Conclusion

"You only need permission from yourself."

That's not just the title of this book. It's a truth you've carried deep in your bones, perhaps unspoken, perhaps buried, but present all the same. If you've made it to this final chapter, then you've done something extraordinary. You've chosen to sit with your story. To confront the truths that many avoid. To face not only the pain of your past but also the possibility of your future.

This journey wasn't meant to give you a brand-new set of rules or a step-by-step life formula. It was meant to offer you something far more powerful: **a way back to yourself.** A reclamation. A reminder that the version of you that you were always meant to be was never lost, only layered beneath survival, conditioning, fear, and expectations that never belonged to you in the first place.

You didn't need this book to be told what to do. You needed it to hear what's been whispering inside you all along: *You are allowed to live freely, fully, and honestly, as you are.*

A Message From My Heart

This book wasn't written for applause, algorithms, or approval. It was written from a place of deep remembering. Every chapter, every sentence was born out of a moment I once lived. This is the version of me I needed when I was scared, confused, unseen, and silently aching for someone to say, "Me too."

I wrote it for the girl I was at 14—lying in a hospital bed, wondering if my life would ever feel like it belonged to me.

For the version of myself who drank charcoal to survive, but didn't yet know how to live. For the woman walking miles while raising a child on her own, holding onto dreams no one else could see, refusing to let go even when everything around her screamed, "Give up."

I wrote it for you—for the reader who has felt invisible in crowded rooms, loud in their silence, tired of performing strength and desperate to be held.

You've survived so much. Not just the obvious pain—but the quiet wounds. The misunderstandings. The betrayals behind smiles. There is pressure to be everything to everyone while barely being seen at all. And still, here you are. Breathing. Becoming.

You carried generational grief while planting seeds of joy. You tried to build a future even while cleaning up a past you didn't create. Though the world has asked you to shrink a thousand times, you kept rising anyway—even if you rose alone.

But now? It's time to rise with ease.

To rise with softness.

You should rise not because you have to prove something but because it's your birthright to live fully.

The Core Messages We've Walked Through

Over these chapters, you've been invited to look closely at the parts of yourself that have long needed tending. Let's reflect on what you now carry:

- **Healing is not reserved for the chosen few. It is your birthright.** You were never meant to survive merely; you were meant to live with intention, clarity, and joy.
- **Self-love isn't a trend—it's your foundation.** Everything you create, give, and become flows from how deeply you believe in your own worth.
- **Your boundaries are not punishments—they are love in action.** They declare, "I know what I need, and I am worth protecting."
- **Solitude does not equal deficiency.** Being on your own does not mean you're incomplete—it means you are powerful enough to hold space for yourself.
- **Your story is not your shame.** What happened to you doesn't define you. What you build from it does.
- **You do not need anyone's permission to become.** Not your parents. Not your church. Not your partner. Not your past. That power has always lived within you.

You've read about the silent wars people wage inside themselves. The impact of emotionally unintelligent people. The heartbreak of abandonment. The deep ache of trying to heal in spaces that refuse to acknowledge harm. And you stood on every page without turning away. That matters. That courage is not small.

But the real question now is this: ***What will you do with what you've learned?***

A Personal Note to the Reader

Let me say this gently, in case the world has been too loud:

You are not behind.

You are not broken.

You are not too late.

You are in process.

You are in bloom.

You are unbecoming everything that was placed on you and remembering everything that was placed *in* you.

The voice in your head that tells you to wait?

To earn?

To prove?

That voice is not your intuition—it's your conditioning.

You don't have to wait for someone to clap before you take the stage. You don't have to collect permission slips to live your truth.

You already have everything you need to begin. So start the business. Take the trip. Leave the room that keeps shrinking you. Say the words you've rehearsed in your head but were afraid to speak out loud.

And yes, there will be people who won't understand.

Who won't cheer? Who will question your change?

That's okay.

Because I'm clapping for you.

For every time you got back up.

For every time you chose peace over proving.

For every time you gave yourself what no one else knew how to offer you.

You are not too much.

You are not unlovable.

You are not a mistake.

You are a walking permission slip.

And it's already signed.

Final Reflection Prompts

- What would you do tomorrow if you truly believed you were allowed to?
- What part of your story have you kept quiet, not out of privacy, but out of shame?
- What is your why for healing? What future are you fighting for?

- What does real freedom look like for you—and are you willing to step into it without apology?
- Who are you without the weight of other people's expectations?

Final Prayer

God,

Thank You for walking with me through every chapter—especially the ones I thought would break me. Thank You for reminding me that I was never too far gone to come home to myself. That my voice still matters. That my life still matters. That I am still becoming.

Let the lessons I've lived turn into light for someone else. Let the parts I thought were scars become the seeds of healing for generations after me. Help me to trust my voice.

To honor my truth. To choose myself—not in rebellion, but in reverence.

And on the days I forget who I am, whisper it back with holy clarity: You only need permission from yourself.

Amen.

www.ingramcontent.com/pod-product-compliance
Lightning Source LLC
LaVergne TN
LVHW010914110826
845149LV00013B/2360
9798993880853